"Bailey and Wills deserve our thanks for compiling a wonderful set of sermons on the practice of Christian ministry. Edwards's preaching is so edifying, his example so instructive, that I wish this book were required reading for all who serve in Christian ministry."

DOUGLAS A. SWEENEY
Chair, Department of Church History and the History of Christian Thought,
Trinity Evangelical Divinity School
Author of *Nathaniel Taylor, New Haven Theology, and
the Legacy of Jonathan Edwards*

"I agree profoundly with Charles Colson's assessment that 'the western church . . . desperately needs to hear Edwards's challenge.' Mercifully God keeps on making that possible with fresh transcriptions of Edwards's preaching. Here are nine more sermons we have never seen before. And what do we find? More shocking juxtapositions that shake us out of our banal generalizations about God. Like: 'In that it was God's own blood, it was the blood of one that had been from all eternity infinitely happy.' Though the title of this collection is *The Salvation of Souls*, it was Edwards's way to say 'the salvation *and happiness* of souls.' Look for it in these sermons! He knew better than most of us that God is not honored by people who pursue salvation from hell but do not pursue happiness in God. Edwards will have none of it, and neither should we. These sermons will help free us from worn and powerless language."

JOHN PIPER
Senior Pastor,
Bethlehem Baptist Church, Minneapolis
Author of *God's Passion for His Glory: Living the Vision of Jonathan Edwards*

"In a day when massive numbers of Christians are biblically illiterate and theologically blind, there is a critical need for both preachers and pew-sitters to read sermons from a master. Thanks are due to Richard Bailey and Gregory Wills for making these unpublished sermons available to a wide audience."

GERALD R. MCDERMOTT
Author of *Jonathan Edwards Confronts the Gods* and
One Holy and Happy Society: The Public Theology of Jonathan Edwards

"Amid a clamor of voices advising pastors, Jonathan Edwards's voice rings clear with biblically sound and Christ-centered advice. Bailey and Wills have done pastors, students, and scholars a great service by making these fine sermons available and accessible."

STEPHEN J. NICHOLS
Lancaster Bible College

"*The Salvation of Souls* represents a unique contribution to the large and still growing field of Jonathan Edwards scholarship. Here for the first time are previously unpublished sermons of Edwards in a single volume. Although Edwards is best known as a theologian, this collection will make clear his sense of preaching as the Christian minister's highest calling. This should be indispensable reading for seminarians, ministers, and church groups interested in engaging America's greatest philosopher, theologian, and pastor. The editors are to be congratulated for their authoritative work in transcribing and editing a notoriously difficult hand, and presenting texts to the twenty-first-century reader in an accessible manner. All in all a splendid achievement."

HARRY S. STOUT
Jonathan Edwards Professor of American Christianity,
Yale University

"The excellent introduction and painstaking editing of these nine previously unpublished special-occasion sermons have provided us a treasure. There is a graced piquancy here that comes from their landmark occasions. *The Salvation of Souls* makes penetrating reading for both pastor and congregation."

R. KENT HUGHES, Pastor, College Church,
Wheaton, Illinois

"Unbelievably, despite oceans of academic and popular attention, many of the manuscripts and notes from Jonathan Edwards's sermons remain unpublished to this day. Thus, Richard Bailey and Gregory Wills perform a special service in bringing this set of sermons on the ministry to print. The voice of Edwards here is calmer and more reflective than in his famous (though rare) sermons of hellfire and damnation. The words, however, are clear, the biblical anchor direct, and the message (especially of God and his grace in Jesus Christ) compelling."

MARK A. NOLL, McManis Professor of Christian Thought , Wheaton College,
Wheaton, Illinois

"This resource is a gem for scholars interested in Edwards's preaching and ministry. And it lets Edwards's words of comfort and challenge be heard once again by church leaers and congregations."

AMY PLANTINGA PAUW
Henry P. Mobley, Jr. Professor of Doctrinal Theology
Louisville Presbyterian Theological Seminary

THE SALVATION OF SOULS

SALVATION

of

SOULS

*Nine Previously Unpublished Sermons
on the Call of Ministry and the Gospel by*

JONATHAN EDWARDS

Edited by
RICHARD A. BAILEY & GREGORY A. WILLS

CROSSWAY BOOKS

A DIVISION OF
GOOD NEWS PUBLISHERS
WHEATON, ILLINOIS

The Salvation of Souls

Copyright © 2002 by Richard A. Bailey and Gregory A. Wills

Published by Crossway Books
    A division of Good News Publishers
    1300 Crescent Street
    Wheaton, Illinois

Cover design: Josh Dennis

Cover photo: Courtesy of the Billy Graham Center Museum, Wheaton, IL.

First printing, 2002

Printed in the United States of America

Library of Congress Cataloging-in-Publication Data

Edwards, Jonathan, 1703-1758.
    The salvation of souls : nine previously unpublished sermons on the call of ministry and the gospel by Jonathan Edwards / edited by Richard A. Bailey and Gregory A. Wills.
        p. cm.
    Includes bibliographical references and index.
    ISBN 1-58134-451-1 (TPB : alk. paper)
    1. Clergy—Office—Sermons. 2. Sermons, American—18th century.
3. Congregational churches—Sermons. I. Bailey, Richard A., 1974-
II. Wills, Gregory A. III. Title.
BV662 .E39   2002
253—dc21   2002010701

LB		13	12	11	10	09	08	07	06	05	04	03	02
15	14	13	12	11	10	9	8	7	6	5	4	3	2	1

FOR
PAUL R HOUSE AND C. BEN MITCHELL,
*two of "those truly wise that shall shine as
the brightness of the firmament."*

Contents

FOREWORD

by

George M. Marsden

Jonathan Edwards was first of all a preacher. His central concern, as the editors of this volume point out, was the salvation of souls. At the center of his own experience was the encounter with God best encapsulated in his famous sermon "A Divine and Supernatural Light." Those who are recipients of the saving grace of God are given "eyes to see" the beauty of the love of God manifested in the saving work of Christ on the cross. Once people glimpse that beauty and love, they are inexorably drawn to it. As when one recognizes any overwhelming beauty, one cannot help loving it at the same time that the love is wholly voluntary. So it is with the mysterious power of God's saving grace that allows one to see what is truly beautiful and lovely. The job of the preacher is to use God's Word as a means of awakening people at least enough to look for the love and beauty that their sins keep them from apprehending or (in the case of the converted) from apprehending fully.

In the midst of the debates over the Great Awakening, Edwards made a revealing comment about the effects of preaching. During intense periods of awakenings, evangelists often preached to the same audiences daily, or even more frequently. Opponents of the awakening argued that people could not possibly remember what they heard in all these sermons. Edwards responded that "The main benefit that is obtained by preaching is by impression made upon the mind in the time of it, and not by the effect that arises afterwards by a remembrance of what was delivered."[1] Preaching, in other words, should be designed primarily to awaken, to shake people out of their blind slumbers in the addictive comforts of their sins. Though only God can give them new eyes to see, preaching should be designed to jolt the unconverted or the converted who doze back into their sins (as all do) into recognizing their true estate.

Edwards's emphasis on the immediate affective impact of preaching might seem surprising from reading some of these sermons. By today's standards, they may seem calmly intellectual. They are thoroughly organized, point by logical point. They have few emotive images. None is anything like "Sinners in the Hands of an Angry God." Partly their seemingly staid nature is due to the occasions for which they were preached. Several are ordination sermons, for instance. Yet these sermons are far more typical of Edwards's usual preaching than is "Sinners," with its elaborate piling up of vivid images. The power of most of Edwards's sermons was in their logic. His goal was to make an impression "upon the mind" of a hearer. The mind, he believed, was the most important seat of the affections. Purely intellectual knowledge was incomplete. True knowledge must involve the affections, which shaped one's heart, will, and hence one's actions.

Though deceptively simple-looking in their organization and unadorned instructive style, Edwards's sermons often could have a strong affective impact. "The Kind of Preaching People Want," for instance, involves a skillful turning of the tables on critical parishioners. Once hearers grant Edwards's unassailable premise that God's Word, rather than human lusts, should be the norm for good preaching, they are forced to recognize that they stand condemned by their own usual resistance to gospel preaching. This sermon offers a message of which more recent generations of pastors and congregations need to be reminded. Other sermons are more simply instructive, such as "Deacons to Care for the Body, Ministers for the Soul," which reveals Edwards's characteristically strong distinction between body and soul. At the same time, his comparison of the church's works of mercy with Old Testament duties of sacrifice provides a powerful lesson, still applicable today. Edwards's sermon on "Ministers to Preach Not Their Own Wisdom but the Word of God," although seeming to have less affective potential, is nonetheless a fascinating summation of his views of faith and reason. While granting a large place for reason as a source of truth, he insists that the dictates of reason must be tested by Scripture, rather than the reverse. Probably one of the most emotionally powerful of the sermons when it was first delivered was that on Acts 20:28, preached at the ordination of Edward Billing in 1754. Both Edwards and Billing had been dismissed by their congregations. For Edwards his dismissal from Northampton was the most emotionally devastating experience of his life. He knew that Billing must have also suffered miserably. Edwards's theme for the sermon is that "Christ's expending his own blood for the salvation and happiness of the souls of men" should be a model for ministers. His thoroughgoing exposition of the many implications of this remarkable truth might seem overly theoretical if viewed in the abstract. If viewed in its setting, however, of the suffering that everyone knew each minister had endured for matters of principle, the cumulative emotive impact could be substantial.

Whatever the subject, the personal intensity of Edwards's otherwise undramatic preaching style reflected his deep commitment to all that he was saying and was therefore often deeply affecting to his hearers.

In all, this collection of sermons is a valuable addition to the available literature on Edwards. Its focus on the ministry makes it particularly valuable for pastors (but also to those who listen to pastors) who are open to guidance from other eras in understanding their divine errand.

NOTES

1   Jonathan Edwards, *Some Thoughts Concerning the Present Revival of Religion in New England*, in Edwards, *The Great Awakening*, ed. C. C. Goen, Vol. 4 of *Works of Jonathan Edwards* (New Haven, CT: Yale University Press, 1972), 397. I am indebted to Timothy Keller for pointing out this passage.

INTRODUCTION

by

Richard A. Bailey & Gregory A. Wills

In these sermons, all of which have never been published (except for one—"Ministers to Preach Not Their Own Wisdom but the Word of God," in the *Southern Baptist Journal of Theology* [Volume 3, Number 2, Summer 1999]), Jonathan Edwards (1703-1758) defines the nature and task of the minister of the Gospel. At bottom, Edwards's position is straightforward. The primary work of the ministry is saving sinners.

Edwards's influence on American Christianity was extensive, and his thought has enduring appeal. He integrated the "New Learning" of the British Enlightenment—its empiricist approach to human knowledge and its psychology—into a Christian worldview. He bolstered Calvinist theology before the growing popularity of Arminianism. He promoted a piety of the heart in opposition to formal and rationalist religion. His preaching and writing was the catalyst for the Great Awakening, and he developed an influential theological defense of the revival. At the heart of his work, however, was his aim to save sinners. He explains in these sermons that Jesus came into the world to save sinners, and he sends out his ministers to do the same.

EDWARDS'S CAREER AS A MINISTER OF THE GOSPEL

Edwards steadfastly applied himself to the task of the ministry. For most of his career he served the congregation at Northampton, Massachusetts, from 1727 to 1729 as assistant to his grandfather

Solomon Stoddard, and from 1729 to 1750 as sole pastor. At Northampton he labored successfully to save sinners. For about six months in 1734 and 1735, Northampton experienced a remarkable revival in which virtually the whole town grew concerned about their eternal welfare, and many professed saving faith. When Edwards described this event in his *Faithful Narrative of the Surprising Work of God*, published in 1737, he hoped that the story would prompt others to pray and preach for the salvation of sinners. The book succeeded and set the stage for the vast transatlantic revival that followed. When the Great Awakening kindled in 1740 through the conversionist preaching of itinerant George Whitefield, Northampton and the Connecticut River Valley participated fully. Edwards played a leading role and encouraged the awakening by preaching and publication.[1]

Edwards's zeal for the salvation of sinners was central to his vision of the ministry, but the church's mission entailed more than conversion and evangelism. Christ ordained that his people should pursue righteous lives and should keep the church pure. In 1749 Edwards concluded that by admitting professedly unconverted persons to Communion, the church had compromised the purity of Christ's ordinance. He informed the church that henceforth he would offer the Lord's Supper only to persons who had professed faith and whom the church judged in charity to be converted. This reversed the church's practice under both Stoddard and Edwards himself, in which all persons who assented to the doctrine of the church and pledged to live moral lives could receive Communion. New England churches had debated the question before, but by the 1740s most Congregationalists saw Edwards's new view as a disruptive innovation.

Although Edwards argued at length that his position was scriptural, he convinced few. In 1750 the congregation dismissed him by a large majority. From 1751 to 1757 he served in Stockbridge on Massachusetts's western frontier as pastor to the colonists and as missionary to Native Americans. He became president of Princeton College in 1758 but died later that year from a smallpox inoculation.

EDWARDS'S VISION OF THE WORK OF THE MINISTRY

In the sermons published here, Edwards explains that the task of the ministry was given by God. Ministers, he asserted, are on a divine errand. God has not authorized them to choose their duties or their doctrines. "Ministers are only sent on his errand. God has not left it to their discretion what their errand shall be." The errand of ministers is to save sinners by preaching the Gospel. They are unequal to the task. But those who labor faithfully and look to God for success generally receive God's blessing. Those who fall prey to the many dangers that beset the ministry face a frightful prospect.[2]

The errand is divine. "Ministers of the Gospel," Edwards said, "are sent forth by Christ." To be sent, ministers must have an "external call to work," in which Christ's church formally sets them apart to the work. But the Spirit of Christ must also call them inwardly, by which Edwards meant primarily that Christ inwardly inclined and disposed them to the work of the ministry.[3]

The errand is comprehensive. God has issued instructions on the nature and duties of the office of minister. Through the apostles Christ ordained the organization of the church, including its officers, government, worship, and discipline. The apostles organized the first churches at Christ's command. The Jerusalem church in the book of Acts, Edwards held, "is set forth as a pattern for all other Christian churches in its constitution." The example was normative.[4]

The apostolic churches established two kinds of officers in the church. They established deacons to look after the physical needs of the church, and bishops, also known as pastors or elders, to look after the spiritual needs. The pastor is a minister in Christ's kingdom.

As "Christ's officer," he bears the authority of his office. Edwards exhorted Christians to receive humbly the teaching of the ministry from the Scripture, for it was the teaching of Christ, who had inspired the Bible. They should submit therefore to their ministers.[5]

Christ called his ministers to exercise their office faithfully. The faithful minister was to "give up himself to this work with his whole heart, and to give up himself to God in it." They should enter the work not from regard for temporal support or financial advantage, but for the advancement of the kingdom of their Lord and Master and for the good of souls. The ministers of Christ should therefore be ready to "exert themselves and deny themselves and suffer" for these ends. They should be ready to sacrifice all their temporal goods and even their own lives for the sake of Christ's kingdom, should God in his providence require it. Christ and the apostles labored and suffered and died for the kingdom, setting an example for ministers to follow.[6]

To labor for the sake of Christ and his kingdom means rescuing lost souls, Edwards held. Christ's work was the work of redemption, and he sends out his ministers to continue that work. The minister's business, he proclaimed, "is to be an instrument to carry on Christ's work, the work of redemption." Faithful ministers "will labor hard for the salvation of souls."[7]

Ministers save sinners by faithfully preaching the Gospel. Ministers in fact have no power to save. God alone makes the preaching effective for the salvation of sinners. Ministers must therefore depend upon God for the success of their labors. They should not depend upon their abilities, learning, eloquence, reputation, or preparation. If they expect to persuade and convert persons through their own gifts and eloquence, "there is danger that God will withhold his Spirit and then it will all be in vain."[8]

Ministers should instead depend upon Christ and pray for the presence of God's Spirit to make their preaching effective. Ministers cannot produce success—they cannot make sinners repent and believe in Christ. They must attend to faithful administration of the orders Christ committed to them. They must be faithful especially in the ordinance of preaching.

Faithfulness in preaching first means submission to God's Word. Ministers must not employ a rule of interpretation that overthrows Scripture's teaching. What seems right to our reason cannot be made a rule for interpreting Scripture. This would make our own reason a better guide than God's revelation and would effectively overthrow

Scripture whenever reason is dissatisfied with what Scripture reveals.

Faithfulness in preaching also means that ministers are to preach all the doctrines taught in Scripture. God has not left to ministers' discretion what doctrines they should teach their people. They are "to preach the preaching he bids them." God has put into their hands the Bible and sends them to preach its message. "God does not need to be told by his messengers what message is fit to deliver to those to whom he sends them, but they are to declare his counsel and are not to shun to declare his whole counsels, when men will hear or whether they will forbear."[9]

Faithfulness in preaching finally means that preachers are to seek not merely to instruct the mind, but to move the heart. In this Edwards was consistent with the Puritan tradition, which aimed to make doctrine useful, as God intended it to be. And so he brought the truth to bear on the consciences of his hearers. He rebuked and exhorted and warned. He reminded his hearers frequently that death must come upon all and that it would come shortly. He warned them to put away their sins lest the preaching of the Gospel be in vain toward them and they fail to escape condemnation in hell.

Although faithfulness in itself has "no sufficiency or efficacy to obtain success," yet God usually blesses the labors of faithful ministers, Edwards said. And even if ministers have little success, if they are faithful, they will not forfeit a glorious reward.[10]

The congregation has a vital interest in sustaining a faithful ministry. "A good minister that has the presence of God with him in his work," Edwards taught, "is the very greatest blessing that God ever bestows upon a people, next to himself."[11]

The congregation must do their part to make the ministry a success. Edwards warned his hearers of their duty in salvation: "If you continue to live careless, unawakened, and slothful in the business of religion, you never will be saved, let you have what minister you will. . . . If you should live under the most eminent minister that ever lived, it will only aggravate your damnation." The people must receive the preaching of the Word and embrace it in their hearts in personal repentance, faith, and holiness.[12]

The congregation must also support their minister in order to advance the success of his ministry. They should give him an adequate and comfortable salary. They should seek to avoid all strife between minister and people. The two were related. Edwards felt nothing promoted "uneasiness and contention between a minister and people" more than failure adequately to support the minister. Such strife undermined the aims of ministry and was a worse calamity, Edwards felt, than a "war with the Indians." It was worse because at risk were spiritual goods, not temporal goods. "People that keep their minister low in the world and oppose him in his work and weaken his hands do but fight against their own souls and undermine their own everlasting welfare." A successful ministry redounded to the everlasting gain of the people.[13]

The congregation must also protect the scriptural purity of the ordinances of the Gospel. This included all the matters Christ had ordained in the church. The greatest need, Edwards felt, was in the area of church discipline. "There is no other part of the ministerial work more unfavorable and attended with greater difficulties." It was the people's duty to "stand by their minister in the regular exercise of church discipline, both that it may be made easy to him and that it may be effectual and successful in its issue."[14]

But the work of the ministry was in any case attended with "a great many difficulties," Edwards judged. Many congregations in fact failed to provide adequate support for their minister. Many contended with their minister and did not support attempts to sustain the purity of the ordinances. In it all, Edwards held, "the devil tries to hinder ministers all that ever he can."[15]

Edwards himself experienced these things. As noted above, when he tried to persuade his Northampton congregation that they were not administering the Lord's Supper scripturally, because many unqualified persons were receiving it, they did not support him. The resulting contention led to his dismissal.

But the suffering of faithful ministers was little compared to that of unfaithful ministers. On judgment day even the condemned will testify against unfaithful ministers for their failure to seek the salvation of souls. Such ministers neglect the proper work of the ministry and attend chiefly to accumulating wealth. They will face a dreadful judgment. "Those precious souls that were committed to our care lost through our neglect," Edwards warned, will "rise up in judgment against us and shall declare how we neglected their souls."[16]

But God will condemn unfaithful ministers also out of their own mouths. They "little think how they are drawing up their own indictments when they are composing their sermons." Ministers are in the best position to know God's will and are under the greatest obligations to do it. Among the wicked, Edwards admonished, no "order of men whatsoever will have so low a place in hell [as] unfaithful and wicked ministers." They will endure a "distinguished torment."[17]

PREACHING AND THE MINISTRY IN EDWARDS'S DAY

Edwards's sermons represented the traditional Puritan model in most respects. Puritan sermons began with a brief "opening" or explanation of the scriptural text. Then came the first "doctrine" of the text, which the preacher explained and defended. He then drew spiritual applications of the doctrine, called "uses." Each sermon typically advanced several doctrines, and each doctrine had several uses.

Edwards's sermons differed from this model in one respect. Edwards typically advanced only one doctrine from the sermon's text.

Edwards, like the Puritans generally, sought "plain" preaching, free of rhetorical ornament and refined eloquence. Puritan preachers did not, however, eschew all rhetorical devices or tropes. They approved the use of restrained figures of speech such as metaphor or personification. Edwards was at times daring nevertheless. He did not attempt the grand style, but he could use a simple literary device in a grand way with remarkable effect. The sermon below on Micah 2:11 ("The Kind of Preaching People Want") is a good example.

For many years Edwards took a complete sermon manuscript into the pulpit. About the time of the Great Awakening, he began relying on briefer outlines. Although in later life he regretted his reliance on notes in the pulpit, he never overcame it. His voice was not strong, but his speech was distinct and precise. He did not preach in a wooden or detached manner, but with a gravity, sincerity, and zeal that carried power. He conveyed emotional ardor and theological insight by his choice of words more than by the character of his delivery.[18]

Edwards believed that the ministry was in jeopardy in his day. The spread of rationalist and Arminian views of religion threatened it on the one side, and the proliferation of spiritualist and anti-establishment Separatists threatened it on the other.

Many in New England no longer preached the true Gospel, Edwards held, and instead advanced Arminian notions of human nature and salvation. They aimed their eloquent essays at the moral instruction of the mind, not at the conversion of the heart. Reason was the road to virtue, they held, not impassioned appeals to the heart. When the awakening spread in the 1740s, such preachers accused Edwards and his fellow revival preachers of reducing religion to emotional excitement at the expense of reason.

Edwards addressed both threats. Faithful ministers, he held, must preach the Gospel in its Calvinistic understanding. They must aim at the heart, not merely at the mind. Arminian preaching would lead to the disappearance of "saving religion." It pleased God on the contrary to visit revival on plain Calvinistic preaching. When Edwards preached against Arminianism in his 1734 sermons on justification by faith alone, God made them especially an instrument of awakening and converting many souls. The success of gospel preaching depends upon the favor of God, not the wisdom or eloquence of human reason.[19]

Against the Separatists he argued that the ministry must retain the dignity and authority of its office. Ministers are called by Christ. In setting ministers apart from the laity, Christ placed distinct duties upon ministers. He committed the teaching and ordinances of the church to their administration.

The laity among the Separatists sometimes took the ordinances of the ministry into their own administration. They especially practiced "lay exhortation." Although technically distinct from preaching, this involved lay exhorters in publicly instructing the people in doctrine. By way of defense, they typically pleaded that their settled minister was unconverted and did not preach gospel truth. But Edwards argued that the prerogatives of the ministry ought not in any case be seized by laypersons.[20]

Ministers of the Gospel today must negotiate their way amid a multitude of voices urging a perplexing variety of models for ministry. Edwards developed a persuasive vision of the nature of the ministry and of the church from its central task of rescuing the lost. Around this central task revolve the other tasks and ordinances of the ministry and the church. God is glorified as Christ gathers his redeemed into faithful and virtuous congregations in which ministers preach the whole counsel of God's Word and exhort their hearers to maintain the purity of their lives and of the church. Edwards's voice still compels across the years. The work of the ministry is saving sinners.

PREPARING THE TEXT

The task of deciphering Edwards's handwriting is notoriously difficult. His sermons present a particular challenge. The first challenge is the orthography itself, which Edwards scholar Thomas Schafer characterized as "exasperatingly formless."[21] Other challenges include elliptical constructions, irregular capitalization, cramped interlinear alterations, and the absence of helpful punctuation.[22] We have throughout sought to reproduce the texts as Edwards wrote them in his sermon notebooks. Some changes were necessary, however.

We have modernized Edwards's spelling. We have spelled out his shorthand symbols and abbreviations, such as ampersands and "thems [themselves]." We have rendered contractions in their full-word forms (for example, we substituted "has not" or "have not" for Edwards's "han't," "be not" for "ben't," "it is" for "tis"). We rendered the abbreviations "i.e." and "viz." as "that is" and "namely" respectively. We retained many archaic usages (such as "aspeaking" and "abegging") but have modernized verb forms (such as "does" for "doth" and "has" for "hath") and a few other archaic forms (such as "begrudge" for "begrutch" and "going to warfare" for "going a warfare"). To accord with modern pronunciation, we substituted "a" for "an" in several places. In two places we changed verb number to achieve subject-verb agreement. We have introduced most of these without comment.

All punctuation and capitalization is that of the editors. We consulted the patterns of capitalization, punctuation, and paragraph division exhibited in Edwards's works that he prepared for publication. Kenneth Minkema, Executive Editor of Yale University's *Works of Jonathan Edwards* series, rendered much gracious assistance by making extensive suggestions in these areas.

We have otherwise followed the very sensible conventions of the *Works of Jonathan Edwards* series.[23] We thus follow their conventions for numbering the heads and subheads of the sermons, for regularizing Scripture citations, and for indicating any words that we have inserted. Square brackets ([]) indicate words that either in our opinion Edwards inadvertently omitted or that are necessary to make sense to the modern reader. Curly brackets ({}) indicate an ellipsis and enclose those words that Edwards deliberately omitted in order to save himself the trouble of writing out the entire phrase. Edwards typically indicated an ellipsis by a long dash. In most cases the phrase he intended presents no difficulty, but in some cases it is less certain. Where Edwards indicated that a Scripture passage was to be read but did not write the passage, we have inserted the passage from the version Edwards used, the King James Version. In places where Edwards wrote out a Scripture passage, we have left it as Edwards wrote it.

ACKNOWLEDGMENTS

Several persons deserve special thanks for their help in this project. The staff at the Beinecke Rare Book and Manuscript Library of Yale University, where all of these manuscripts are housed, assisted graciously in early stages of our research. Margaret Freeman of the Hadley Historical Commission, Hadley, Massachusetts, directed us to information regarding Chester Williams, the town's third permanent pastor. The *Southern Baptist Journal of Theology* published an earlier version of the sermon on 1 Corinthians 2:11-13 in article form. Ken Minkema applied his experienced editorial hand throughout the transcription and editing of these sermons, affording us the benefit of his expertise and friendship. With gracious enthusiasm, George Marsden agreed to take time away from his forthcoming biography of Jonathan Edwards to write the foreword, sharing his keen historical judgment. Marvin Padgett, Lane Dennis, and the Crossway Books staff encouraged our work from the outset. With love and support, Leanne Bailey endured several trips to New England, accompanying Richard in both libraries and cemeteries. Cathy, Sam, Abby, James, and Maggie Wills reminded Greg of the things more important than wrestling with Edwards's punctuationless prose. Finally, Paul House and Ben Mitchell, to whom we dedicate this volume, entertained and encouraged us, as well as serving as instruments of edification.

NOTES

1 To learn more of Edwards's life and thought, see George Marsden's forthcoming biography of Edwards (New Haven, CT: Yale University Press, 2003); Stephen J. Nichols, *Jonathan Edwards: A Guided Tour of His Life and Thought* (Phillipsburg, NJ: P & R Publishing, 2001); Iain H. Murray, *Jonathan Edwards: A New Biography* (Carlisle, PA: Banner of Truth, 1987); Conrad Cherry, *The Theology of Jonathan Edwards: A Reappraisal* (1966; reprint, with a new introduction by the author and a foreword by Stephen J. Stein, Bloomington, IN: Indiana University Press, 1990).

   To read more from Edwards's sermons and writings, see John E. Smith, Harry S. Stout, and Kenneth P. Minkema, eds., *A Jonathan Edwards Reader* (New Haven, CT: Yale University Press, 1995); Wilson H. Kimnach, Kenneth P. Minkema, and Douglas A. Sweeney, eds., *The Sermons of Jonathan Edwards: A Reader* (New Haven, CT: Yale University Press, 1999); and the splendid multi-volume *Works of Jonathan Edwards* published by Yale University Press, each volume of which includes excellent introductory materials.

2 "Ministers to Preach Not Their Own Wisdom but the Word of God."

3 "The Minister Before the Judgment Seat of Christ."

4 "Deacons to Care for the Body, Ministers for the Soul."

5 "Pastor and People Must Look to God."

6 "Pastor and People Must Look to God"; "The Work of the Ministry Is Saving Sinners."

7 "Pastor and People Must Look to God"; "The Minister Before the Judgment Seat of Christ."

8   "Ministers Need the Power of God."

9   "Ministers to Preach Not Their Own Wisdom but the Word of God."

10   "The Minister Before the Judgment Seat of Christ."

11   "Pastor and People Must Look to God."

12   "Pastor and People Must Look to God."

13   "Pastor and People Must Look to God"; "The Minister Before the Judgment Seat of Christ."

14   "Pastor and People Must Look to God."

15   "Preaching the Gospel Brings Poor Sinners to Christ."

16   "The Minister Before the Judgment Seat of Christ."

17   "Pastor and People Must Look to God"; "The Minister Before the Judgment Seat of Christ."

18   For discussion of Edwards's approach to preaching, see Wilson H. Kimnach, "Jonathan Edwards' Art of Prophesying," in Edwards, *Sermons and Discourses 1720-1723*, ed. Kimnach, Vol. 10 of *Works of Jonathan Edwards* (New Haven, CT: Yale University Press, 1992), 1-258; and Richard A. Bailey, "Driven by Passion: Jonathan Edwards and the Art of Preaching," in *The Legacy of Jonathan Edwards: American Religion and the Evangelical Tradition*, eds. D. G. Hart, Sean Michael Lucas, and Stephen J. Nichols (Grand Rapids, MI: Baker, forthcoming 2003).

19   See Edwards's letter to the Northampton Church (June 1752), in Edwards, *Letters and Personal Writings*, ed. George S. Claghorn, Vol. 16 of *Works of Jonathan Edwards* (New Haven, CT: Yale University Press, 1998), 484; Edwards, *A Faithful Narrative of the Surprising Work of God in the Conversion of Many Hundred Souls in Northampton*, in Edwards, *The Great Awakening*, ed. C. C. Goen, Vol. 4 of *Works of Jonathan Edwards* (New Haven, CT: Yale University Press, 1972), 148-149; and Goen, "Editor's Introduction," in ibid., 17-21.

20   See, for example, Edwards's letter to Deacon Moses Lyman, May 10, 1742, in Edwards, *Letters and Personal Writings*, 102-103; and Edwards, *Some Thoughts Concerning the Present Revival of Religion in New England*, in Edwards, *The Great Awakening*, 83-88.

21   Thomas Schafer, "Manuscript Problems in the Yale Edition of Jonathan Edwards," *Early American Literature* 3 (1969): 166.

22   See Helen Westra's colorful characterization of the difficulties in *The Minister's Task and Calling in the Sermons of Jonathan Edwards* (Lewiston, NY: Edwin Mellen Press, 1986), 49, note 24.

23   For the conventions of the *Works of Jonathan Edwards*, see Wilson H. Kimnach, "Note to the Reader," in Edwards, *Sermons and Discourses 1720-1723*, ed. Kimnach, Vol. 10 of *Works of Jonathan Edwards* (New Haven, CT: Yale University Press, 1992), xi-xii.

1

EDITORS' INTRODUCTION

THE DEATH OF FAITHFUL
MINISTERS A SIGN OF
GOD'S DISPLEASURE

Edwards preached this sermon when the people of Northampton were grieving the deaths of some of the town's leading men. Solomon Stoddard, Northampton's pastor since 1672, died February 11, 1729. Ebenezer Strong, a long-time ruling elder in the church, died the same day. Strong was the last ruling elder to be chosen in Northampton. Additionally, many were grieving the death of Rev. John Williams of Deerfield, Massachusetts, who died on June 12.[1] Williams was Edwards's uncle and had many relatives in Northampton. He had preached there at the funeral of Solomon Stoddard.[2]

Edwards generally judged local calamities to be indications that God was displeased with the people. He interpreted these recent deaths as such a calamity. Many "elders," the righteous pillars of the land, had died. Edwards reminded the people that God had blessed them through Stoddard's ministry and through the revivals that occurred during his tenure. But now religion was declining, family government weakening, and licentiousness spreading among the youth.

The central concept behind the doctrine is that God often blesses a people by raising up righteous leaders, especially ministers, among them. When these die, it is a sign that God is ready to visit his wrath upon the rest if true repentance and reformation are not forthcoming. Edwards established his doctrine by persuasive appeals to Scripture. He argued that God was quickly removing the generation of Stoddard, Strong, and Williams, and few such pillars remained. He exhorted the few remaining "aged ones" to pray for the benighted rising generation and warned the young to emulate the departed pillars lest they bring ruin upon the town.

———

The manuscript, held by the Beinecke Rare Book and Manuscript Library, Yale University, consists of eight duodecimo leaves.

THE DEATH OF FAITHFUL
MINISTERS A SIGN OF
GOD'S DISPLEASURE

ISAIAH 3:1-2

For, behold, the Lord, the Lord of hosts, doth take away from Jerusalem and from Judah the stay and the staff, the whole stay of bread, and the whole stay of water, the mighty man, and the man of war, the judge, and the prophet, and the prudent, and the ancient.

Isaiah was one of the prophets that was sent to forewarn Judah and Jerusalem of their approaching destruction by the Chaldeans. He begins this book of his prophecy with it. In the beginning of the first chapter, God, complaining of their grievous sins, declares to them in the seventh and eighth verses, "Your country is desolate, your cities are burned with fire; your land, strangers devour it in your presence, and it is desolate, as overthrown by strangers. And the daughter of Zion is left as a cottage in a vineyard, as a lodge in a garden of cucumbers, as a besieged city." And it is the same destruction that the prophet is upon here in our text. These words, in their sense, are connected with the last words of the preceding chapter: "Cease ye from man, whose breath is in his nostrils: for wherein is he to be accounted?" They were warned to have no dependence upon their mighty men and their men of war, nor upon their teachers, nor rulers, nor those men noted for wisdom and experience, for his "breath is in his nostrils." And more especially at this time had they need to beware that they did not trust in men, however prudent and mighty they are, and however useful they have been, because God was about to take away such from amongst them.

We find an account of a remarkable fulfillment of this prophecy in the history we have in Scripture of the desolation that God brought upon Judah and Jerusalem. 2 Kings 24:14-16, "And he carried away all Jerusalem, and all the princes, and all the mighty men of valor, even ten thousand captives, and all the craftsmen and smiths: none remained, save the poorest sort of the people of the land. And he carried away Jehoiachin to Babylon, and the king's mother, and the king's wives, and his officers, and the mighty of the land, those carried he into captivity from Jerusalem to Babylon. And all the men of might, even seven thousand, and craftsmen and smiths a thousand, all that were strong and apt for war, even them the king of Babylon brought captive to Babylon." They were only the dregs of the people that were left, after their mighty and prudent men [were taken away] and those that were publicly useful with respect to the people's civil and temporal concerns. God also took away their prophet, for when upon this [occasion] the king of Babylon made Zedekiah king instead of Jehoiachin, Zedekiah shut up Jeremiah, the prophet that God had sent to warn them, in prison, and afterwards cast him into the dungeon, as we have an account in the thirty-seventh and thirty-eighth chapters of Jeremiah. And there were other prophets [such] as Ezekiel [and] Daniel.

And there was an exact fulfillment also of what we have in the fourth verse, where God says that he will give children to be their princes and babes to rule over them, as the governors were that afterwards obtained the rule over them, as appears by the history we have of them in Jeremiah.

DOCTRINE

It is a manifestation of God's displeasure against a people when he takes away from them many that have been useful and serviceable amongst them.

The text speaks of a removal—captivity and death both—for many of them were slain in battle as well as multitudes carried captive. But we shall insist only upon a removal by death. *Proposition I.* When persons are removed from amongst a people by death, it is God [who] removes them. Not but that there may be second causes, as there were second causes of the captivity of the children of Israel; and yet it is said in our text, "Behold, the Lord, the Lord of hosts, doth take away."

God fixes every man's limits and designs the particular time of his death. The number of every man's months and days and hours are with God; they are written in his book. Job 14:5, "Seeing his days are determined, the numbers of his months are with thee, thou hast appointed his bounds that he cannot pass." When God brings a child into the world, he brings it and places it here to live here for so long a time; though God does not reveal the time beforehand, yet he appoints and fixes it unalterably. Every man has his time appointed as much as a hireling. When men are hired to work, they are often hired for a day or for a fixed time; so God fixes every man's time in the world. Job 14:6, "Turn from him, that he may rest, till he shall accomplish, as an hireling, his day"; and 7:1, "Is there not an appointed time to man upon earth? Are not his days also like the days of an hireling?"

Therefore the time of man's life is compared to the day or time of the sun's continuance above the horizon. Christ says, "I must work while the day lasts: the night cometh, when no man can work" [John 9:4]. Because as the limits of the natural day are unalterably fixed—all the world cannot alter it if they would ever so feign; they cannot retard or accelerate the sun in its motion—so none can alter the appointed time of man's life.

Indeed, God determines whatsoever comes to pass and orders all things by his providence. But a more special providence appears in his ordering of some things, and the time of man's death is one. There is not so great a connection between this effect and any second causes within our reach or within our knowledge as there are in many other things. We have not our lives in our own hands, but they are in God's hands. Whatever care persons may use to preserve and lengthen out their lives, yet death will oftentimes surprise men when they had no expectation of it. When diseases come that prove mortal, it is because God sends them. They are commissionated by him to do their work of cutting asunder the thread of [life]. When fatal accidents happen, they are of God's ordering. Death is God's messenger that he sends in his time to summon men to appear before his judgment seat. When persons lose men and dear relations, it is because God takes away. He called them out of the world at such a time because it seemed meet unto him. In this matter, he acts as sovereign of the world, and gives none account why he does so.

Proposition II. God, in fixing the term of persons' lives, oftentimes has respect to the people amongst whom they dwelt. The God that knows all things and is a being of infinite wisdom has many things in view in his providences. He has, in the first place, respect to his own glory: He fixes a person's bounds in such a place because he intends thereby to glorify himself. And he has also a respect to man in such providences. He has especially respect to the person himself in determining {the term of his life}. God often takes away wicked men, when in the midst of doing impiety, in his wrath; and because he will repay them to their faces, it is threatened that wicked men shall not live out half their days. God takes away wicked men because they have filled up the measure of their sin; they have sinned as much as God sees meet they should be allowed. And in fixing the death of the godly at such a time, it is sometimes a frown of God and a manifestation of his displeasure for some sin of theirs—as in the death of Moses and Aaron—and oftentimes in mercy to them he takes them away from the evil to come.

But God has not only a respect to the persons themselves—they be not the only persons concerned—but God has respect to others that survive, that are to consider such dispensations as what respects them—and not only mere relations, but others also with whom they have dwelt and been conversant. God speaks to the living, and he intends that they should hear and understand his voice. Thus men are greatly blamed for not considering and laying to heart the death of righteous men. Isaiah 57:1, "The righteous perisheth, and no man layeth it to heart: and merciful men are taken away, none considering that the righteous is taken away from the evil to come." God has respect to the state and behavior of a people in such providences as these amongst them.

Proposition III. It is a manifestation of God's displeasure.

Men may be publicly useful many ways. Various kinds of usefulness are mentioned in the text and following verse. Those are very useful that well execute public offices, that are faithful to trust reposed in them. Some are very useful to a people with respect to their civil interest. Good rulers and judges are benefactors: They are ministers of God to a people for good and are a terror to evildoers and a praise to them that do well; they are the defense of a people, the foundation pillars of a community (Psalm 82:5).

Wise and faithful ministers of the Gospel are very useful men. They are use[ful] to a people in those things that concern their greatest interests, even the eternal salvation of their souls.

And men that are men of wisdom and a good spirit are publicly useful, whether they are in any public place or no. They may have many opportunities of doing good in the places where they dwell. Men of good understanding, prudence, and virtue are great blessings. They may be useful in discountenancing vice and wickedness, in promoting good designs, in appearing on the side of right. They may greatly promote those things that are commendable only by showing that they favor them. They may be useful by their instructions and by their examples. [They] may improve their estates to good purposes.

Truly godly men are always useful and blessings to a people. These stand in the gap, and for the sake of these God sends down blessings on a people. A truly godly man, however mean, may be a great blessing to those he dwells amongst by his presence and prayers and examples.

And especially will a good understanding and moral prudence and public-spiritedness and godliness and a true Christian spirit and zeal for God's glory and the interests of religion, joined together, make a man eminently useful.

When God takes away those that are in these ways useful, it is a manifestation of his displeasure, and especially when he multiplies such breaches upon a people. The following considerations may make us more sensible of it:

First. It is an awful dispensation of God towards a people at any time to cause death to prevail amongst them, much more when he thereby removes many of those that have been particularly useful and serviceable. It was a dismal calamity to the whole people of Israel, and a token of God's terrible displeasure, when he slew so many by the pestilence in David's time. Though we do not know such as had been particularly serviceable were taken more than others, death is an awful thing, and when it is frequent amongst a people, it is a sign an angry God is amongst them. It is a judgment we find often threatened for the wickedness of a people. God shows his anger when he smites a people with death, though but in the inferior members; much more therefore when he smites them in the head.

Second. Useful men are some of the greatest blessings of a people. To have many such is more for a people's happiness than almost anything, unless it be God's own gracious, spiritual presence amongst them; they are precious gifts of heaven. And therefore,

Third. The removal of such often opens a door for great calamities to ensue. It often opens a door for great temporal calamities. So did the death of Joseph: The people lived in peace in Egypt as long as he lived, but when he died, their terrible bondage ensued. There arose another king that knew not Joseph, that dealt cruelly with the people (Exodus 1:8).

It is sometimes followed with great spiritual calamities. Vice and wickedness prevail, and religion and virtue die and are kicked out of doors. Thus it was upon the death of Joshua and the elders that were contemporary with him. Judges 2, from the seventh to the twelfth [verses]:

And the people served the Lord all the days of Joshua, and all the days of the elders that outlived Joshua, who had seen all the great works of the Lord, that he did for Israel. And Joshua the son of Nun, the servant

of the Lord, died, being an hundred and ten years old. And they buried him in the border of his inheritance in Timnath-heres, in the mount of Ephraim, on the north side of the hill Gaash. And also that generation were gathered unto their fathers: and there arose another generation after them, which knew not the Lord, nor yet the works which he had done for Israel. And the children of Israel did evil in the sight of the Lord, and served Baalim: and they forsook the Lord God of their fathers, which brought them out of the land of Egypt, and followed other gods, of the gods of the people that were round about them, and bowed themselves unto them, and provoked the Lord to anger.

And so it was from time to time afterwards. When God raised up judges, they would serve the Lord all the days of the judge; but when the judge was dead, they departed from him again, as in the eighteenth and nineteenth verses: "And when the Lord raised them up judges, then the Lord was with the judge, and delivered them out of the hand of their enemies all the days of the judge: for it repented the Lord because of their groanings by reason of them that oppressed them and vexed them. And it came to pass, when the judge was dead, that they returned, and corrupted themselves more than their fathers, in following other gods to serve them, and to bow down unto them; they ceased not from their own doings, nor from their stubborn way."

A people commonly are much as the leading and principal men amongst them are. And when such of those as have been well-spirited are removed, there is danger lest it should be [of] ill consequence with respect to the morality and religion of a people.

Fourth. God sometimes takes away such as have faithfully served their generation from the evil to come. He sometimes takes them away to make way for the evil to come; he takes away the pillars, that the building may fall and be destroyed. Useful men are as the wall of a people, and when they are removed, the wall is broken down and destruction comes in.

And sometimes God takes them away that they may have no share in those public calamities that he intends shortly to bring upon them (Isaiah 57:1). When God declared to Josiah, through Huldah the prophetess, that the Lord would bring destruction upon that people, God encouraged him that he should not see the evil that God would bring upon that place. 2 Kings 22, from the fifteenth verse:

And she said unto them, Thus saith the Lord God of Israel, Tell the man that sent you to me, Thus saith the Lord, Behold, I will bring evil upon this place, and upon the inhabitants thereof, even all the words of the book which the king of Judah hath read: because they have forsaken me, and have burned incense unto other gods, that they might provoke me to anger with all the works of their hands; therefore my wrath shall be kindled against this place, and shall not be quenched. But to the king of Judah which sent you to enquire of the Lord, thus shall ye say to him, Thus saith the Lord God of Israel, As touching the words which thou hast heard; because thine heart was tender, and thou hast humbled thyself before the Lord, when thou heardest what I spake against this place, and against the inhabitants thereof, that they should become a desolation and a curse, and hast rent thy clothes, and wept before me; I also have heard thee, saith the Lord. Behold therefore, I will gather thee unto thy fathers, and thou shalt be gathered into thy grave in peace; and thine eyes shall not see all the evil which I will bring upon this place.

Therefore when God takes away many such persons from a people, it is to be looked upon as a great calamity and a frown of heaven upon a place or people. And it has a very threatening aspect, and that although many of them may be old. The ancient are one of those kinds of persons mentioned in our text that God threatened to take away from Judah and Jerusalem. Joshua and the elders that outlived him were old when they died, and yet their death was a great calamity to that nation. And God took away his own presence with them, and the people upon it fell into great spiritual and temporal evils.

APPLICATION

The improvement I shall make shall be with particular respect to God's late dealings with us of this town.[3]

I. We of this town have reason to be greatly humbled under the late rebukes of providence of that kind. God has lately taken away many such persons from amongst us that in their day were particularly serviceable in this place. God has taken away the prophet, that eminent minister of the Gospel[4] that God so long continued in this place, that you were wont to hear instructing and warning you from this pulpit. God has taken away him that was as it were the father of this people, that hath begotten you through the Gospel and brought you up, most of you, from your cradles. It has pleased God not long since to put out that burning and shining light; it will shine no more amongst us. By that stroke God cut in sunder our main pillar, and not only so but one of the main pillars of the land.[5]

And with the prophet God has taken away from us the mighty man, and the man of war, the judge and the prudent and {the ancient}. Most of these characters met in him: He was judge, prophet, prudent, ancient. And God has taken away many others lately from us, unto whom some of these characters belonged; his hand has been stretched out upon us for a considerable time, and God has done a great deal towards emptying the town of those that have been in times past pillars in it.

God has taken away our Joshua, he that was our captain to lead us into the heavenly Canaan, and with him he has taken away many of the elders that were contemporary with him.[6] It looks darkly upon us that those of that generation are taken away so fast, and that there is no more hopeful prospect from the rising generation.

Licentious and immoral practices seem to get great head amongst young people. And how little appearance is there of a spirit of seriousness and religion to be seen among them. How little concern about their salvation and escaping eternal misery. How few that seem to be earnestly inquiring what they shall do to be saved. How little is religion in credit amongst many of them, but [they] rather pursue those vanities, [in] which there is great danger that they will prove to the eternal ruin of their own souls and the ruin of the place.

When a generation lives in a way of hardened vice and wickedness all the while they are young, there is no great prospect of there being much religion amongst them when they are risen. Particular persons may become serious and religious and truly godly, but a generation that are very vicious when rising will not probably be very religious when risen.

And except God wonderfully appears, this portends mischief to future generations. They that live loosely while young and give the reins to their lust, it is to be feared they will not hold the reins very taut with respect to their children. When a people have got into a way of declining, they will be likely to wax worse and worse, to revolt more and more. It is like a falling stone: The further it descends, the more strongly does it incline to descend.

There has been much of the presence of God seen in this town in times past; there has been much of a spirit of religion to be seen.[7] But we have reason to fear that as the former generations are gathered to their fathers, the other generations which will rise, which have not known the Lord nor seen the mighty works which he has wrought for Israel, will forsake the God of their fathers. And then we can expect no other than that all manner of calamities will come in like a flood upon us, and we shall be a ruined people. "Righteousness exalteth a nation, but sin is a reproach to any people" [Proverbs 14:34].

Surely therefore we are called upon this day to humble ourselves under the mighty hand of God when he is thus manifesting his displeasure against us and threatening us. Let us look upon it as a reality that God is displeased with us.[8]

And let us consider what we have done to displease [God], wherein we have provoked God to anger and what share we have had in drawing down such judgments of God against us. It should now be everyone's work to reflect on himself, to view his past life, to be looking into his own heart and turning his feet into God's testimonies.

II. Let the godly that remain amongst us be stirred up to strive earnestly with God, that he would yet dwell with us; that he would turn from the fierceness of his anger and lift up the light of his countenance upon us; that he would turn [to] us again and cause his face to shine [upon us], so that we may be saved, as they see God taking away persons that have been long useful in this place; that [we] should be the more earnest that God would raise up others; that [we] may be of a good spirit and that [we] shall set good examples and seek the peace of Jerusalem.

Particularly, that young people may be led wisely to consider their latter end and see the necessity they stand in of a savior and may many of them be turned savingly unto God.

And that God would be with him that he has placed here in the work of the ministry, that he would instruct him and give him much of his Spirit and grace and give him success in his administrations, that he may yet see much of the goodness of God to this people. Particularly, I would beseech and exhort those aged ones that yet remain, while they do live with us, to let us have much of their prayers, that when they leave the younger generations, they may leave God with them.

III. Let all that have the interests of the town at heart do what in them lies that those that are the rising generation may be useful in their generation, particularly by a careful and painful educating of their children and government of their families. There begins the ruin and there begins the making of a people, in family education and government. If everyone would do his duty this way, there would be a great prospect of good unto this people.

IV. You that are young, be careful that you be not the reproach of your generations. Others are going off, and you, those of you that are to live (for it is not probable that all of you are to live till you are past your youth), I say you that are to live are coming on endeavors to make good the ground of those that have gone before, that you may not have a hand in ruining the town. There are some men [who], instead of being public blessings, are public nuisances. Ecclesiastes 9:18, "One sinner destroyeth much {good}." They cumber the ground. Instead of being useful members in society, they are like a cancer in the body. Take heed that it be not so with you.

NOTES

1   *The* (Boston) *Weekly News-Letter*, June 19, 1729, 3.

2   John Williams, *Death of a Prophet Lamented and Improved* (Boston, 1729). Also see Patricia J. Tracy, *Jonathan Edwards, Pastor: Religion and Society in Eighteenth-Century Northampton* (New York: Hill & Wang, 1979), 29.

3   Edwards deleted with a diagonal line: "I. Hence we learn that we have great
     cause to lament the death of such persons. We are to lament it not only as we
     are great losers by it, but as it is a manifestation of God's displeasure."

4   That is, Solomon Stoddard, who served Northampton from 1672 until his
     death in 1729.

5   Edwards deleted the following passage with a vertical line: "He was one that
     was endued with all qualifications that should render a person eminently use-
     ful amongst a people, being endued with great abilities and understanding,
     great prudence, great experience, a great zeal for the public good, especially
     for the greatest good of a people, the good of their souls. He was a person of
     great piety, and he was in such a public station as gave the greatest advantage
     to be useful. And thus, by that one blow, God took away the judge, the
     prophet, and the ancient."

6   Among the "pillars" who died in 1729 were Rev. John Williams of Deerfield,
     Massachusetts, who died on June 12, 1729, and ruling elder Ebenezer Strong,
     who died on February 11, 1729, the same day as Stoddard.

7   In *A Faithful Narrative of the Surprising Work of God*, Edwards related that under
     Stoddard's preaching, Northampton had experienced revivals in 1679, 1683,
     1690, 1712, and 1718. See Edwards, *A Faithful Narrative of the Surprising Work
     of God in the Conversion of Many Hundred Souls in Northampton*, in Edwards, *The
     Great Awakening*, ed. C. C. Goen, Vol. 4 of *Works of Jonathan Edwards* (New
     Haven, CT: Yale University Press, 1972), 145.

8   Edwards deleted with a diagonal line: "You may be ready to argue secretly in
     [your] hearts after this manner: 'How do I know that God takes away such and
     such persons in anger to the living? They live till they are old and according
     to the ordinary course of nature. It is no wonder that they lived no longer.'"

2

EDITORS' INTRODUCTION

MINISTERS NEED
THE POWER OF GOD

In 1729 the Northampton, Massachusetts, church lost their pastor of fifty-seven years, Solomon Stoddard. They chose his young grandson, Jonathan Edwards, to succeed him. Although Edwards had been Stoddard's assistant for two years, there was much uncertainty in the change. Stoddard had led the church successfully, and God had blessed his preaching with spiritual awakenings. Neither Edwards nor the congregation knew whether God would similarly bless his ministry.

Edwards charted a course for his ministry in this sermon in which he addressed the uncertainties. God's Spirit and power had accompanied Stoddard's ministry, Edwards said, and the people should now pray that the same might accompany his own ministry. Edwards's conviction that God, not the minister, determined the success of ministerial labors was central to his view of the ministry. Edwards saw ministers as "earthen vessels" in the hands of the Almighty, who uses them for his own glory. He asserted that ministers are "utterly insufficient" to carry on the work of God's grace.

Edwards felt his own insufficiency. He apparently delivered this sermon at the time of his installation as pastor in Northampton. He was still a relatively inexperienced pastor at the age of twenty-six. But for twenty years he proved a worthy successor to Stoddard, until the church dismissed him in 1750 because he demanded stricter standards of admission to the Lord's Supper. In 1729, however, with his career at Northampton in its earliest stages, Edwards chose a sermon that might establish his ministry on the necessity of God's blessing and presence if he and his congregation hoped to see the work of God's grace.

As he developed his doctrine, Edwards moved from the insufficiency of ministers, who are the instruments God uses, to the sufficiency of God to accomplish his purposes through such jars of clay. Edwards exhorted his Northampton congregation to depend on God alone, and not on past ministers, such as Stoddard, or on present ministers, such as Edwards. Ministers are to be loved and honored by their people, but only as the instruments God uses to accomplish his good pleasure.

The manuscript, held by the Beinecke Rare Book and Manuscript Library, Yale University, consists of seven extant octavo leaves. There is evidence in the text, seen in misnumbering, that one or more leaves have been lost.

MINISTERS NEED
THE POWER OF GOD

2 CORINTHIANS 4:7

But we have this treasure in earthen vessels, that the excellency of the power may be of God, and not of us.

In the preceding chapter the apostle is magnifying his office as minister of the Gospel, and he does it by setting forth the gloriousness and spirituality of the Gospel and that dispensation that he was a minister of. He compares it with the former dispensation by Moses, showing how much more glorious it was than that, as in the seventh and following verses of that chapter: "But if the ministration of death, written and engraven in stones, was glorious"; and, "how shall not the ministration of the spirit be rather glorious"; and, "if the ministration of condemnation be glory, much more doth the ministration of righteousness exceed in glory"; and, "if that that is done away was glorious, how much more that that remaineth is glorious."

He also shows how much more clear and plain the gospel dispensation is than that that was in types and shadows. This is the plain manifestation of the thing typified; verse 12, "we therefore use great plainness of speech." Moses put a veil over his face to hide the glory and brightness that appeared in it. But we, under the Gospel, "with open face behold the glory of the Lord," as [also in] verses 13 and 14.

He also in this chapter makes profession of his faithfulness in his handling of so glorious a dispensation. He professes that he had renounced the hidden things of dishonesty and did not handle the Word of God deceitfully, did not preach himself but Christ Jesus, as in the second and fifth verses.[1] "For," says he, "God, who commanded the light to shine out of darkness, hath shined in our hearts, to give the light of the knowledge of the glory of God in the face of Jesus Christ," and it is that that puts me upon preaching the Gospel, and not any worldly or selfish consideration. The same, in other words, as is in the thirteenth verse: "As it is written, I have believed, and therefore have I spoken; we also believe, and therefore speak."

And that he might not seem to seek his own honor either by preaching the Gospel or thus extolling the Gospel which he preached, he says in our text, "We have this treasure"—that is, this ministration of the Gospel which is so much more glorious than that of Moses, this light of the glory of God in the face of Jesus Christ— "in earthen vessels, that the excellency of [the] power may be of God, and not of us."

Earthen vessels are the meanest sort of ware, and the weakest, the most frail and brittle. As if he had said, "We are [in] no way worthy to have that that is so glorious as the Gospel of Christ Jesus committed to our charge, to receive so high and excellent an office, to be the keepers of so great a treasure. Nor are we in ourselves any way sufficient to manage it, weak and altogether without strength. If we were left to ourselves, this treasure would be lost in our keeping, as that that is contained in earthen vessels is in danger of being lost by the vessel's breaking."

The apostle was chosen of God [to] be an instrument of setting up the kingdom of Christ through the world. But what is a frail man for such a work? Liable to sickness, persecution, and death, what has he to oppose all the strength and opposition of the world? One blow would put an end to him as well as any other man. He had not the strength of mighty armies to bear all before him, but went about unguarded to resist the opposition and persecution and malice of a wicked and heathenish world. God chose such an instrument, so insufficient of himself, that it might appear that the work was not man's but God's, that the excellency of power might be of God and not of him. And therefore God wonderfully upheld him and succeeded him in the midst of all those troubles and persecutions, as in the verses immediately following the text. "We are troubled on every side, yet not distressed; we are perplexed, but not in despair; persecuted, but not forsaken; cast down, but not destroyed; always bearing about in the body the dying of the Lord Jesus, that the life also of Jesus might be made manifest in our body. For we which live are alway delivered unto death for Jesus' sake, that the life also of Jesus might be made manifest in our mortal flesh. So then death worketh in us, but life in you."

DOCTRINE

That God is pleased to make his own power appear by carrying on the work of his grace by such instruments as men, that in themselves are utterly insufficient for it.

The work of God we speak of is that work of his that respects the souls of men with relation to their salvation. For though all things in creation and providence are the works of God, yet this is a work that [he] more especially concerns himself in and appears in. Here we shall speak to three[2] things: I. Those instruments that God makes use of to do his work are in themselves utterly insufficient for it. II. God does the work. III. Hereby God's own power and influence in this work may appear.

I. Those instruments that God makes use of to do his work in the souls of men are of themselves utterly unable to do it. This inability of the instruments appears from the condition that the soul of man, that is the subject of this work, is naturally in, and from the imperfection of themselves that are made use of as instruments. And as to the state which the soul is naturally in, it may be represented by these three things:

First. It is forsaken of God. The welfare of every creature depends on the presence of its Creator with it. It depends as much on its Creator for its well-being as it did at first to be brought out of nothing. If God forsakes it, it will be immediately in a miserable, perishing condition, as much as a branch when cut off from the vine, or as the member[s] when they [are] separated from the body.

And more especially does the welfare and good state of the soul of man depend on God's presence with it. When God once forsakes it, it is lost and becomes altogether wretched.

But men, as they come into the world, are in a forsaken condition. God is departed from them. His Holy Spirit is taken away, and they are without God in the world.

And therefore ministers are utterly unable to help the soul in the lost condition except they can unite God to it again, except they bring God to them [the lost] and make him dwell with them.

They have no power to help the poor, lost soul except they have power over the Almighty and have him at command. For God is the soul's welfare and happiness, and he only. And as long as he forsakes the soul, it will be in a lost condition. They can as soon create a reflection of the sun['s] beams when the sun does not shine as enlighten the soul of man when God does not shine into it.

Second. Hence, the soul in its natural state is spiritually dead. Ephesians 2:1, "And you hath he quickened, who were dead in trespasses and sins." Colossians 2:13, "And you, being dead in your sins . . . hath he quickened together with him." That is, the soul is so entirely destitute of the first principles of holy and spiritual life that [it is] as much without it as he that is naturally dead is of the principles of natural life. The fire is all gone out. There is not one spark left. It signifies nothing to blow, except fire be brought from some other place.

Surely physicians are, of themselves, none of them able to raise the dead. You may apply what medicines you please to a dead man, you cannot fetch him to life. You may set what food you will before him, it will not nourish him. You may represent what objects you will, he will not see. If you charm in his ears ever so wisely, he will not hear. You can do no good at all to a dead man. Nothing that you do will have influence upon him. So nothing that ministers can do, if God does nothing, can have any influence at all upon the souls of sinners, their conversion or spiritual good.

Third. The soul is naturally in a state of captivity unto Satan. 2 Timothy 2:26, "who are taken captive by him at his will." Man has departed from God and chose rather to serve Satan than him; therefore, God suffered Satan to take possession.

Now, therefore, except ministers are stronger than the powers of darkness, they are utterly unable to deliver the souls of men out of their hands. Ministers are set by God to pull down the strongholds of Satan. But if they are without any other help but their own strength, alas, they are miserable, weak things to go against the prince of the power of the air and to engage the god of the world. The name of Christ himself is celebrated upon the account of that victory which is obtained over the devil, and to conquer him through his own strength is a thing for him to do and not for us. Luke 11:21-22, "When a strong man armed keepeth his palace, his goods are in peace: but when a stronger than he shall come upon him, and overcome him, he taketh from him all his armor wherein he trusted, and divideth his spoils."

II. The inability of the instruments that God makes use of to do his work appears from their imperfections.

First. In that they are creatures and finite beings. If ministers were angels incarnate and had the wisdom and strength of angels and could speak with the tongues of angels, it would be all one [that is, it would make no difference]. If God hid himself and withheld his influence, they would be creatures still, and their power and knowledge would be limited. The highest angel in heaven[3] cannot convert one soul, if God does not set in.

Conversion is the peculiar work of God. There are some works that none can do but God, not men nor angels. Such is creation, and such is raising from the dead, and such is the conversion of the soul, which is both a creation and a resurrection. The grace of God is a gift that never any can bestow but God. It is a jewel that God has in his own keeping and never commits to any but his own Son to bestow.

If ministers knew perfectly the circumstances of every soul, knew all his thoughts and the workings of his heart, and so knew how to suit the word exactly to his case; if he could set forth the Gospel in the most powerful, moving, and convincing manner that the nature of words will allow of, yet if the matter be left there and God does nothing, nothing will be done. The soul will remain dead as before. But,

Second. Ministers are not only creatures, but very feeble and infirm, partakers of the same infirmities as their hearers. Acts 14:15, "Sirs, why do ye these things? We also are men of [like passions with you]."

[III. That hereby God's own power and influence in this work may appear . . .][4]

[*First.* In furnishing means so weak and insufficient . . .]

[. . .] and graces. So that it is evidence that their sufficiency, their ability and accomplishments are not of themselves, but of God, because God is pleased to give them a double portion of his Spirit.

Thus [was it with] Moses, when God was sending him to his people and to Pharaoh. Exodus 3:11, "And Moses said unto God, Who am I, that I should go unto Pharaoh, and that I should bring forth the children of Israel out of Egypt?" Exodus 4:10-11, "And Moses said unto the Lord, O my Lord, I am not eloquent, neither heretofore, nor since thou hast spoken unto thy servant: but I am slow of speech, and of a slow tongue. And the Lord said unto him, Who hath made man's mouth? Or who maketh the dumb, or deaf, or the seeing, or the blind? have not I the Lord?" And God so furnished him afterwards that he became one of the most eminent of God's ministers that ever was here in the world. He was the greatest of the Old Testament prophets.

So the prophet Jeremiah, when God was about to send him upon his message to the children of Israel, complains,[5] "Ah, Lord God! I cannot speak for I am a child." But the Lord said to him, "Say not I am a child. For thou shalt go to all that I send thee and whatever I command thee thou shalt speak." And in the ninth verse we read that God touched his mouth and put his words in his mouth. And how great a prophet he was after this.

And what a marvelous alteration did Christ make in the twelve apostles. When he took them, they were most of them poor, illiterate, ignorant fishermen. And how ignorant and childish were they while Christ remained bodily present with them. But there was an extraordinary alteration made in them at the pouring out of the Holy Ghost in the day of Pentecost, and they were wonderfully furnished unto their work.

Second. In crowning means so weak and insufficient with great success, as God [did] the twelve apostles. He made those poor fishermen the conquerors of the world. By means of their preaching, he subdued the whole Roman Empire and overcame all the opposition that kings and emperors and philosophers could make [against] them. Christians were a poor, despised sort of men, but yet they carried all before them. The gates of hell, by all the power or wit and learning of earth, could never prevail against them. So God despised and disgraced earthly power and wisdom by [the] subjecting of it to those that were so weak and ignorant and showed that the foolishness of God is wiser than men and the weakness of God is stronger than men (1 Corinthians 1:25).

APPLICATION

I. Hence we learn that God does not make use of means because he needs them. What he shows us by producing those great effects is that it [that is, conversion] is dependent only upon the power of God, and that he could as easily do it without any at all, as God makes not use of the ministry of angels because he could not do what they do immediately with equal ease. He sent an angel to destroy the army of the Assyrians that came against Hezekiah, when he could, if it had so pleased him, have destroyed them all by a word's speaking. So God, if he so pleased, could with perfect ease, without any external means at all, instruct, awaken, and convert men. He could have converted the whole Roman Empire at once, without the ministry of the apostles and other ministers, by whom he gradually did it through much opposition and many sore persecutions.

It is upon many accounts an instance of the wisdom of God to make use of means in this work. It is a method much more agree-able to our state and circumstances here in this world, a way wherein there is more opportunity and occasion for the exercise of diligence, and that renders the unconverted more inexcusable—and those that diligently use the means of grace may obtain a glorious reward—a way that gives great opportunity for the manifestation of God's wisdom in the ordering of the affairs of his church and for the gradual display of gospel truth and [the] confounding of his ene-mies, et cetera.

II. Hence we learn that it is a great honor that God does men when he makes them the instruments of work wherein God's power is so much manifested. It is an honor to the angels to be employed in such glorious messages as they are employed in. It was a great honor to the prophets and apostles that God made them the instruments, or rather the occasions, of working such miracles that were immensely beyond the strength and wit of man. It was a very great honor God did Moses, that at his word such wondrous miracles should be wrought, and so too Elias.

But this work is a far more glorious work than those miracles. There is more of the power and wisdom and grace and other perfec-tions of God seen in it than in them. Christ reckoned it a greater work. John 14:12, "Verily, verily, I say unto you, He that believeth on me, the works that I do shall he do also; and greater works than these shall he do; because I go unto my Father." How should he do greater works? The apostles nor none of the disciples ever wrought greater miracles than Christ wrought. But doubtless Christ meant that they should do spiritual works of wonder in bringing men from a state of spiritual death to life. And in respect of this, the apostles and other disciples did greater works than Christ himself while upon earth. Christ's preaching and miracles while on earth converted but few. But the apostles turned the world upside down.

This is as glorious a work as creation. It is the new creation. How great an honor, therefore, is it that God should make his word in the mouths of men to be a means of this work.

III. Hence we learn who it is we must have our dependence

upon to make the word and ordinances successful, namely, him whose power is manifested in their success. We are not to depend upon ministers that in themselves are so insufficient for so great a work. If we should have our eyes only to God, we should be earnest with him.

Ministers themselves should have their dependence here. They should go to Christ, the great Prophet who calls them and sends them forth to labor in his vineyard. They should not depend upon their own parts, or learning, or eloquence, or on the goodness of their preparations, or in the good opinion that men have of them, but their eyes should be to God. They should look to him to bless them in this great work.

They that are about to undertake this work and devote themselves to it ought to do it with a sense of the greatness of the work and of their own insufficiency for it and of their unworthiness of the honor of being called to and improved in it, and especially being succeeded in it and actually made instruments of carrying on the work of God's grace in the hearts of men. The apostle Paul was often acknowledging the freeness of grace in making him a minister. Romans 1:5, "By whom we have received grace and apostleship, for obedience to the faith among all nations, for his name." So in the beginning of many of his epistles, he attributes his being an apostle to the sovereign will and good pleasure of God. So also Galatians 1:15-16, "But when it pleased God, who separated me from my mother's womb, and called me by his grace, to reveal his Son in me, that I might preach him among the heathen." He reflects on his own unworthiness. 1 Timothy 1:12-13, I thank God through Jesus Christ "who hath enabled me, for that he counted me faithful, putting me into the ministry; who was before a blasphemer, and a persecutor, and injurious." 1 Corinthians 15:9-10, "For I am the least of the apostles, that am not meet to be called an apostle, because I persecuted the church of God. But by the grace of God I am what I am."

Those that are about to undertake this work should do it with the greatest seriousness and consideration of the vast importance of the work, how great a thing it is to have the care of precious souls committed to them, and with a suitable concern upon their minds, considering the great difficulties, dangers, and temptations that do accompany it. It is compared to going to warfare (1 Corinthians 9:7; 1 Timothy 1:18). They ought solemnly to devote themselves to the Lord to serve him in this work, with a resolution to give themselves wholly to these things, and with all their might to seek the advancement of Christ's kingdom and the salvation of souls in it, looking to God to furnish them with those gifts and graces of his Spirit that shall fit them for this work, for these are the fruits of God's grace. 1 Corinthians 3:10, "According to the grace of God which is given unto me, as a wise masterbuilder, I have laid the foundation, and another buildeth thereon. But let every man take heed how he buildeth thereupon." So it is of the grace of God that ministers are assisted diligently and laboriously to improve these gifts and graces in their work. 1 Corinthians 15:10, "I labored more abundantly than they all: yet not I, but the grace of God which was with me." It is the fruit of the grace of God that ministers are faithful in their work. 1 Corinthians 7:25, "as one that hath obtained mercy of the Lord to be faithful."

And [ministers] should beg of God that his Spirit may accompany their administration. If their own abilities and performances are but mean, yet if they have a true love to souls and desire of advancing the kingdom of Christ, God is able to make the weapons of their warfare mighty to the pulling down of strongholds, as he made David that appeared so weak and insufficient a warrior to prevail over Goliath without sword or shield or spear, with only the instruments of a shepherd.

And if they have never so great strength of natural power, and never so great gifts, yet if they depend upon their own abilities and look that everyone should be persuaded and converted by their gifts and eloquence, there is danger that God will withhold his Spirit, and then it will all be in vain.

It is to God that a people are to have their eye in so great an affair, as what they are nearly concerned in, as well as their minister, whom they are about to settle. The ordinances of God among them is the greatest and most important affair that a people can be concerned [in], and it is highly becoming them earnestly to look to God on such an occasion. The people of Israel had their direction when they were about to build the sanctuary. 1 Chronicles 22:19, "Now set your heart and your soul to seek the Lord your God; arise therefore, and build ye the sanctuary of the Lord God, to bring the ark of the covenant of the Lord, and the holy vessels of God, into the house that is to be built to the name of the Lord."

And they should earnestly seek God's blessing upon themselves, that they may do their duty wherein concerned in this affair; that they may faithfully do their duty towards their minister; that there may always be maintained an entire peace and love between them and their minister; that they may suitably honor and maintain him and do what is incumbent on them to encourage and assist him; that they may with proper reverence and diligence attend to his administration and receive him as a minister of Christ, and that he may come to them in the fullness of the blessing of the Gospel of Christ.

It is to God also that the people should have their eye, and to him they should make their prayer for a blessing upon their minister's labors. They should look to God that he would every way furnish their ministers with gifts and graces and wisdom and strength for their work, that he would give them much of his Spirit, and that he would give them much of his Spirit through his Word.

And let us be exhorted at this day to look to God for his blessing upon means of grace, that though God has removed one that [had] much of his Spirit and[6] whose administration he was wont to accompany with so much of his Spirit, that he would still make the excellency of his power to appear by the success of remaining means, that he would make it to appear that he is able to do the greatest things by the feeble instrument. Let us, all of us, earnestly pray that he would give us a great treasure, though it be in an earthen vessel.

And let those that are concerned for their salvation seek to God only to convert and save them. Do not trust in your own endeavors, nor in the endeavors that ministers use for you. Do not seek to physicians more than unto God, the great physician of souls. Make God your [counselor] in your difficulties and doubts. Cry day and night unto God for his mercy, for you are in his hands. See that you remember that whenever the great work be wrought in your soul, it must be God that does it.

IV. Let us give all the glory to God when there is any success of the Gospel. This is what God designs by giving the treasure to earthen vessels, that we may acknowledge the treasure to be from God and not from the vessel itself, as we should be ready to think if the vessels were golden vessels.

Ministers should take heed when their labors are succeeded, not to glory in it as if it was because they are better and more able than others. They should not glory in their parts or holiness or zeal, but should attribute it all to God. And the people should look beyond the instruments. Although it is required that they should love them and honor them much for their work's sake, yet they should take heed that they do not attribute that to them which is to be attributed to God only. The people at Lystra were ready to adore Barnabas and Paul for the miracles they wrought, and they took them for gods and brought oxen and garlands and were going to offer sacrifice to them. But when Barnabas and Paul heard of it, they rent their clothes, and running in amongst the people, cried out, "Why do ye these things? We are men of like passions with you" (Acts 14:12[-15]).

And those particular persons that have been converted by means of the administration of God's ambassadors should give the glory to God. They are obliged greatly to love and honor those God has made their spiritual fathers and the instruments of their new birth. But God only should be loved and honored by them, as being he that wrought it in them according to his own good pleasure.

NOTES

1   Edwards deleted with a diagonal line: "And that it may not appear as if the apostle exalted himself by thus magnifying the gospel that was committed to him."

2   Edwards wrote "two" but added a third point.

3   Edwards deleted with a horizontal line: "Michael himself."

4   The leaf(s) with the first part of the third heading is missing.

5   Edwards's manuscript added, "Chapter 1, verse 6."

6   Edwards deleted with a horizontal line: "who he was wont to bless." Edwards undoubtedly had Stoddard in mind.

3

EDITORS' INTRODUCTION

THE KIND OF PREACHING
PEOPLE WANT

Edwards preached this sermon in November 1733, at a time when his congregation was in the early stages of the revival that swept Northampton in 1734 and 1735. At this time he rebuked the young people in particular for pursuing a worldly course on Sundays. The adolescents of Northampton recognized the errors of "mirth and company-keeping" and thoroughly reformed their lives in the manner Edwards suggested. He saw this as the first indication that God was beginning a remarkable work in the town.[1]

In this sermon he rebuked the entire congregation. He decried the many worldly preoccupations of his listeners. In a strikingly rhetorical sermon, Edwards aimed at the consciences of his hearers by assaying the extent to which their hearts took more pleasure in wicked and worldly matters than in spiritual treasures in Christ. Although Edwards did not shrink from direct rebuke, here he begins more subtly. The rebuke derives from reflections on the minister's task. He defined this task negatively, by telling what it is not. The minister's task is not to discount the danger of sin, nor to proclaim a savior who countenances sin, nor to instruct men on how to satisfy their sinful desires, nor to tolerate sin, nor to offer a heaven of worldly pleasure. On the contrary, the business of the minister is to denounce sin as an affront to the righteousness of God.

———

The manuscript, held by the Beinecke Rare Book and Manuscript Library, Yale University, consists of ten duodecimo leaves. The symbol for Edwards's "History of Redemption" project appears in the upper left-hand corner of the first page. Edwards envisioned this unfinished theological project, formally titled *A History of the Work of Redemption*, as his *magnum opus*, covering the grand scheme of God's work on earth in historical order.[2] In the upper right-hand corner of the first page appears the preaching date, "Novem[ber] 1733."

THE KIND OF PREACHING
PEOPLE WANT

MICAH 2:11

If a man walking in the spirit and falsehood do lie, saying,
I will prophesy unto thee of wine and of strong drink; he
shall even be the prophet of this people.

We have an account in the sixth verse how the people treated the true
prophets. They rejected and disliked their prophecies. "Prophesy ye
not," say they of them that prophesy. They disliked the prophecies
of them that God sent to them because they reproved them for their
sins and discountenanced their corruptions and denounced [that is,
pronounced] God's judgments for their judgment. They hated their
prophecies because they were against their sins. If they had behaved
themselves as they ought to do, the word of God would not have
been against them. As it is said in the seventh verse, "Do not my
words do good to him that walketh uprightly?"

In the text it is declared what kind of prophet would suit them,
namely, one that walking in the spirit and falsehood lied, saying, "I
will prophesy unto thee of wine and of strong drink." Such a prophet
as this would be well received and entertained by the people and be
such a one as they would like. They did not like a prophet that
always kept reproving them for their sins and contradicting their
lusts and would not allow them to gratify their sensual appetites, nor
let them have the peaceable enjoyment of their sinful pleasures.

But if there should come a prophet among [them] walking in the spirit and falsehood and should prophecy to them of wine and strong drink, that would fall in with their corruptions and flatter them in their sinful inclinations, that, instead of prophesying of God's judgments for their sins, should foretell sinful pleasures and prophesy of the gratification of their lusts, this would be the prophet that would suit them.

The children of Israel had both these kinds of prophets among them. They had true prophets that reproved them for their sins and denounced against them God's wrath in case they did not repent. These they hated and persecuted.

And they had false prophets that always flattered them in their sins. These were always well entertained and caressed by them. Isaiah 30:9-10, "That this is a rebellious people, lying children, children that will not hear the law of the Lord: which say to the seers, See not; and to the prophets, Prophesy not unto us right things, speak unto us smooth things, prophesy deceits."

DOCTRINE

If the business of ministers was to further the gratification of men's lusts, they would be much better received by many than they are now.

As particularly,

I. If ministers were sent to tell the people that they might gratify their lusts without danger; if they were sent to tell them that it was lawful for to them to gratify their lusts; if they came from God with that message that men might freely use strong drink when they had a strong appetite to it, or that it was lawful for persons to give a lease to the lusts of uncleanness, and that they might allow of unclean practices and might freely enjoy their lascivious pleasures, how eagerly would they be listened to by some, and what good attention would they give. So if they were sent to declare that it was lawful for men, when they had opportunity, to overreach their neighbor in their bargains, or that it was lawful for men to revenge upon their enemies, that it was lawful for them to talk against and reproach [and] revile them that they did not like; or if they were sent to tell them that such things were but little sins, that God did not look upon them as very heinous nor was much provoked by them; if they were sent to tell men that the punishment of such sins was not very great, that it was such as they might well enough endure, or that the punishment was but temporary and not eternal; or if they were sent to tell them that if men did gratify their lusts, there was not danger but that they might easily obtain pardon and forgiveness, that God would be easily moved and persuaded to forgive them if they asked for it, though they gave themselves never so full swing in gratifying their sinfulness; if ministers were sent to tell men that God was such a God that he could not have the heart to take men and cast them into eternal burnings, if they did earnestly beg of him to spare them, that though they spend all their lives in drunkenness or lasciviousness or cheating and fraud, yet if they did but seem to be sorry for it and send up a few earnest cries upon a death-bed, there would be no danger but that God might be won and his heart drawn to forgive them; if ministers were sent to tell men that there was never the less danger of a man's being converted for his long allowing himself in willful sin, that men that give a lease to their lusts under the greatest lights and most solemn warnings were as likely to be converted and have repentance given them as the most strict and conscientious livers, and that there was no danger of provoking God to give them up to hardness of heart, and that great sinners, the most daring presumptuous sinners did as ordinarily go to heaven as others; I say, if ministers were sent with such messages as these, they would be much better received by many than they are now. They would give more heed to what they said and would like it better, would be abundantly more pleased and taken with it. They would lay it up in their hearts.

If the Gospel that ministers preached was full of such tidings as these, it would be accounted more worthy of the name of Gospel, or glad tidings, than it is now. Now they hear of the Gospel's being glorious, but they can see no glory in it. But then it would appear a ten times more glorious Gospel than it does now.

II. If ministers were sent to offer men a savior that countenanced and encouraged men's lusts; if ministers were sent to tell the people that Christ, out of love to men, was desirous that they should have more liberty to enjoy their sinful pleasures, and that he came into the world for that end, to lay down his life to purchase for men a dispensation for sinning and an indulgence that they might gratify their strong and violent carnal appetites with impunity, and that God would not be angry with them for so doing, nor punish them for it, he would appear to them then a thousand times so glorious a savior as he does now. They would receive him then gladly. Ministers need not stand calling and inviting sinners to come to Christ so long in vain. There would be multitudes flocking to such a Christ as this. They would embrace such a savior as this with all their hearts. Where there is one now that comes to Christ, there would be a hundred. They would not need to have the ministers to spend so much breath to set forth the beauty and excellency of Christ, and the necessity of him and the excellency of the way to salvation, and urging and entreating men to close with Christ. No, but they would fall in with the proposal at the first word.

Or if ministers were sent to offer Christ only in one of his offices and not in others; if they were to preach Christ only in his priestly office and as a savior from the punishment of sin, and not also in his kingly office as a savior from the power and dominion of sin, and the being [a King] and a Lord to rule in us and over us, they would by many be much better received than they are now. That would be mighty pleasing to men, to be saved from the punishment of sin and yet not saved from sin, but to be allowed to enjoy it and practice it still. They would like a savior that would save them in their sins much better than a savior to save them from their sins.

III. If ministers were sent to direct men how they might fulfill their lusts, they would be much better received by many than they are now. For instance, if ministers were sent to direct people how they might gratify their covetousness, and to tell them of means by which they might grow rich and get abundance of the world, they would be a great deal better received and hearkened to than they are now. They would listen to such directions as these with much greater diligence than they do when the minister directs them how they may get heaven and may obtain everlasting riches. There are many that while the minister is giving rules how men may obtain eternal life commonly have their thoughts in the meantime off from what is said and in the ends of the earth, thinking of other things quite remote from the business, not regarding and many times not knowing what the minister preaches. But if the minister was sent to tell them how to get estates, [they] would hear and mind every word that was said. There are many that sleep now that would hold up their heads then and would keep their eyes fixed on the minister and their hearts intent on what he delivered. There would not be such an appearance of men's laying down their heads upon their seats, as though they would purposely compose themselves to sleep. If ministers were sent from God to tell men how they might probably get great estates, though the means were not at all more probable than the means they now direct to for obtaining heaven, yet many would be a great deal more ready to put the directions in practice. Though there was not an absolute certainty, but only as great a probability of success, as there is of the diligent use of means of grace for obtaining heaven, yet they would mind what the minister said a great deal more and would be more careful to remember it, would not be half so apt to forget it, and would be abundantly more careful to practice their directions in their lives. They would not be half so apt to raise objections against them. They would not object that it was not certain that they should succeed if they did follow them. But if there was a probability of their growing rich by it, they would be willing to run the venture.

If ministers were sent from God to tell people how they might lay up for children and provide good portions, their word would be more heeded and more practiced than when they tell them how they may educate and bring up their children so as very probably to be a means of their eternal salvation and of their being rich and happy forever in heaven.

So if ministers were sent to tell men how they might gratify their pride, how they might obtain honor and advancement among men, how they might get above such and such of their neighbors that they now with an evil eye see to be above them, this would be more pleasing to them by far than to have ministers tell them how they may become the children of God and may hereafter sit with Christ in thrones and be crowned with glory.

If some persons could learn by ministers how to get fine clothes, so as to make a finer show than their fellows, they would hear with greater pleasure and a greater disposition to practice than when the minister tells them how they may be clothed with the righteousness of Christ and may have the ornaments of the graces of God's Spirit and may hereafter come to shine forth as the sun in the kingdom of God.

So if ministers were sent to direct persons how they might gratify their envy, how they might bring it to pass that this and the other person that is above them might be pulled down and be brought into meaner and more depressed circumstances, and how they might be exalted above [them], so that they might have opportunity of vaunting it over them and give them the mortification of seeing them above them and getting their wills of them, or how they might come up with these and those that have offended them that are of a contrary party and do not seek their interest, be not their friends but hate and despise them, men would keep awake to hear such things. Their attention would be more engaged and their practice a great deal more conformable than now it is. Men that often stay at home, as there are some such amongst us, would probably come more speedily to meetings to hear such things whereby they might gratify their lusts and advance their worldly interests.

IV. Some would like ministers better if they would countenance their scandalous indulgences of their lusts rather than to fulfill the rules of Christ with regard to them. They would like it much better to have their wickedness winked at and approved than to have the minister fulfill the rule in openly reproving and rebuking such practices, exercising Christ's discipline for the reforming and humbling [of] them and bearing testimony against such things.

V. If ministers were sent to offer men a carnal and sensual heaven, they would be much better received by many than they are. It is a dull story to men to tell them of pure, spiritual pleasures, of holy delights, of seeing and enjoying God, of enjoying communion with Christ, of spending an eternity in serving and praising God and the Lamb. They do not understand these things. They have no taste nor relish of them. They have no appetite to such a kind of happiness. It would please them a great deal better if ministers were sent to offer to them such a paradise as the Mahometans expect—a heaven of carnal delights where they shall eat and drink and have all the sensual pleasures that they can wish for.

This would be mighty pleasing to many men that loll and sleep while the glory is offered that Christ has purchased with his precious blood. They would much prefer the gratification of their lusts to God and Christ with all their glory and perfection in the full and perfect enjoyment of them.

Here in this world men cannot gratify their lusts without much interruptions and molestation. They are molested by an accusing conscience. And they are molested with many evils and inconveniences that a sensual, luxurious life brings, such as weakness and diseases of body, and shame and disgrace among men, and many other things. But if they had the news sent to them of a sensual paradise hereafter, where they could gratify all their lusts as much as they would without any molestation or allay at all, this they would account worth a hundred such heavens as the Bible tells of.

APPLICATION

I. [One] *use* may be [that] of *self-examination*. Inquire whether it be not so with you as you have heard, whether you are not one that would be more pleased if ministers were sent to declare to men that it was lawful for them to gratify these and those sensual and vicious appetites, or that they might take the liberty without much endangering their souls thereby. If the minister was sent to reveal to you that Christ had died {so that you could gratify your appetites}, would not you be more pleased and give better attention and be more careful to remember and practice? If the minister was sent to direct you {to gratify your lusts, would you not be more pleased}?

Would not a sensual heaven and paradise of carnal delights be more pleasing to you?

There is need that you should be very strict in this inquiry, in order to know your own heart, as there is in all other self-examinations about the prevailing temper and disposition of our own souls. It is to be feared there are many now that hear this thing proposed, that are ready to clear themselves and to say, No, they are not of that number, that indeed are not clear. Therefore, enter a little more carefully and strictly into this inquiry. And particularly inquire,

First. How is it you receive ministers with the message that they do bring to you in the name of the Lord? How do you attend to them in their delivering their message? Are you one that is wont to give diligent attention? Or are you one whose manner [it is] to sit under the preaching of the Word in a careless manner, little regarding what is said, that makes no conscience of keeping your heart intent on what is preached, but do allow yourself to spend great part of the time in thinking of other things that have no relation to the minister's discourse? Are you not one that does allow yourself in sleeping while the minister is preaching the Word of God? Is the Gospel that is preached to you pleasant and acceptable to you, or is it a dull thing, a dead letter? Have not you an enmity against the Gospel for that reason, because it reproves and condemns your lusts? When you hear, do you hear with a design to practice? And are you actually careful to keep in mind what you hear and to put it in practice? Or are you one that does but just give the minister the hearing and go away and think no more of it and give no more heed to it?

Second. Inquire how it has been with you when you have been hearing other things that tended to gratify your carnal inclinations. By this you have something of a trial whether you are one of them that the doctrine speaks of or no. The ministers be not sent to promote the gratification of your lusts, so that you have no trial that way. Yet you hear many things in your conversations among men that do tend to promote [the gratification of your lusts]. If you are better entertained and pleased with what you hear from others of this nature than with the Word of God, you may thereby judge how you would receive ministers if they were sent with a like message.

How is it when you hear an impure story or lascivious song? Do not you listen more to it, give better attention and hear with more pleasure than when you are hearing the Gospel of Jesus Christ preached? Is not your attention more engaged, and are you not better suited when you are hearing talk that tends to gratify your covetousness? When you hear any talking about the market, about land or cattle or bargains that have been made and such like things? Be not you more in your element when you sit talking of such things than when you are hearing of God and Christ and heaven and the glorious benefits of the Gospel? And how is it when you hear talk that tends to gratify your pride and your envy and ill will? When you sit and hear such and such persons reproached and run down and ridiculed, be not you more entertained, and does not the time pass away more pleasantly than when you hear the glorious things of the Gospel preached? Some persons seem never to be better suited and entertained than with such conversation that is taken up in talking against others.

II. [Another] *use* is [that] of *reproof*. If you are one of those spoken of in the text that if ministers were sent to you to further the gratification of your lusts would much better re[ceive their message], then consider the following things:

First. What horrid contempt you cast on God and Christ and heaven, in that you should prefer the gratification of your vile lusts before them, that you would be more pleased and entertained and give better attention to hear that by which your lusts might be gratified than that by which you may obtain an interest in Christ, in his precious blood and glorious benefits, and may have God for your portion; that to have all the glories and perfections of God and a Redeemer set before you is not so pleasing and entertaining to you as to hear of the objects of a carnal appetite; that worldly profit or sensual pleasures, or the gratifications of your envy and revenge, is better to you than heaven. Who can express how wickedly you act in thus despising the infinite majesty and glory and mercy of God and

Christ, the Son of God, and his precious blood. How greatly have you reason to conclude God is provoked by you.

Second. Consider how sottishly and unreasonably you act in thus preferring the gratification of your lust to eternal happiness in heaven, that you are more willing to listen and hearken and put in practice what you hear, that you may get a little worldly gain or gratify a carnal appetite, than when you hear of being saved and brought to the enjoyment of God and Christ forever.

Third. Consider how justly it may be so ordered that you should never get any good by the word preached that you so despise. Seeing you receive it no better, give no more heed to it, take no more delight in it, how justly might it be so ordered that it should never do you any good or be any means of spiritual benefit to you, but that seeing you should not see, and hearing {you should not hear}, and that it should only be a means to harden you and enhance your guilt and your condemnation another day. How justly may God leave you to your lusts that you set so much by. How justly may he leave you to have your portion in them, denying heaven to you that you have so low an esteem of.

Fourth. How grievous it may justly be to any faithful minister of Christ when men no more regard the message they bring to them. What an encouragement would it be to a minister that labors to find out acceptable words and does what in him lies to speak so as to influence and affect his hearers, to see them attentive, willing to hear and learn, accepting of what he delivers with due concern to practice the same. But how grievous may it well be, when a minister does his utmost, to see a congregation seeming to be regardless of what he says, and many of them sleeping [a] great part of the time, and others plainly manifesting a careless, regardless spirit. With what a complaint may such ministers that have been so treated rise up on the day of judgment before their Master that sent them and set them to work, declaring what pains they took and how they labored to their utmost to speak so as to influence and affect their minds, and yet how regardless they were of the message they delivered.

NOTES

1   Jonathan Edwards, *A Faithful Narrative of the Surprising Work of God in the Conversion of Many Hundred Souls in Northampton*, in Edwards, *The Great Awakening*, ed. C. C. Goen, Vol. 4 of *Works of Jonathan Edwards* (New Haven, CT: Yale University Press, 1972), 146-147. Also see Patricia J. Tracy, *Jonathan Edwards, Pastor: Religion and Society in Eighteenth-Century Northampton* (New York: Hill & Wang, 1979), 109-122.

2   See Edwards's letter to the trustees of the College of New Jersey, October 19, 1757, in Edwards, *Letters and Personal Writings*, ed. George S. Claghorn, Vol. 16 of *Works of Jonathan Edwards* (New Haven, CT: Yale University Press, 1998), 725-730.

4

EDITORS' INTRODUCTION

THE MINISTER BEFORE THE JUDGMENT SEAT OF CHRIST

Edwards preached this sermon on November 17, 1736, at the ordination of David White, pastor of the newly organized church at
Lambstown (now Hardwick), Massachusetts, about twenty-five
miles east of Northampton. White remained pastor of the
Lambstown church until his death in 1784.

In this sermon, Edwards addressed the joy that will fill faithful
ministers at the judgment seat of Christ, and the sorrow that will
descend upon unfaithful ministers. Ministers, being sent by Christ,
must render an account to him. Faithful ones will rejoice with Christ,
for their success is his. They will rejoice together on account of the
souls that were saved and made eternally happy by the ministry of
the Gospel. Edwards exhorted White to be faithful in the work of the
ministry, seeing how great a motive to success there is in the prospect
of rejoicing with Christ in heaven. Edwards also urged faithfulness
from a consideration of the horror that unfaithful ministers will face
on the last day. Edwards finally exhorted the congregation to be
faithful in their duties toward their minister, so that they also might
promote his success.

The identification of Edwards as the preacher at White's ordination has not apparently been noted before. Edwards's notation at the top of the first page of this sermon identifies him as Lambstown's preacher of the day on November 17, 1736. The church minutes identify the occasion as White's ordination: "November the 17th 1736. A Church was gathered and imbodied in Lambstown, and the members of the church publicly invited and chose Mr. David White to be their pastor. Accordingly, the same day, the said Mr. David White was ordained Pastor of the Church of Christ in Lambstown by prayer and laying on of hands of the Presbytery."[1]

The manuscript, held by the Beinecke Rare Book and Manuscript Library, Yale University, consists of eighteen duodecimo leaves. On the first line of the first page, Edwards wrote, "Ordination at Lambstown Novem[ber] 17 1736." In the left-hand margin of the first page appears the symbol denoting this sermon was preached again in 1751.

THE MINISTER BEFORE THE
JUDGMENT SEAT OF CHRIST

LUKE 10:17-18

And the seventy returned again with joy, saying, Lord, even the devils are subject unto us through thy name. And he said unto them, I beheld Satan as lightning fall from heaven.

In the preceding part of the chapter we have an account of Christ sending forth the seventy disciples to preach the kingdom of God and to confirm their word by miracles. He sends them forth as laborers into his harvest; as it is expressed in the second verse, ["Therefore said he unto them, The harvest truly is great, but the laborers are few: pray ye therefore the Lord of the harvest, that he would send forth laborers into his harvest."] In these verses we have an account of their return to their Master after they had been forth on the message on which he sent [them] and had been laboring in the work that he had set them about. Concerning which, we may observe three things:

1. How they are affected on this return to Christ. They returned with joy. Very probably when they went forth, they went with heaviness and fear upon their hearts in consideration of what Christ had told them of the greatness and difficulty of that work that he sent them upon, and the great opposition they should meet with. For Christ told them that he sent them forth as sheep in the midst of wolves. But now, when they had done the work that Christ had sent

them upon and come to meet their Lord again that had sent [them], they come not with heavy but joyful hearts.[2]

2. We may observe the account that they give to their Lord of the events of that embassy that he had sent them upon, and the success they had. "Lord," say they, "even the devils are subject unto us through thy name." They were probably so [that is, successful] in two respects, namely, both as they, by their preaching the kingdom of God as he had commanded, had success in the conversion of sinners and delivering men's souls from the tyranny and dominion of Satan, and they were so as they, by the power that Christ had given them for the confirming of their ministry, had been enabled to cast devils out of those that were possessed with them. For Christ sent them forth not only to preach but to work miracles, to confirm and enforce the word they preached, and this seems to be especially what they mean. In those days when Christ was on the earth, there were multitudes in the land possessed with devils, which seems to have been so ordered to prepare the way for a glorious triumph of Christ over the powers of darkness in casting them out. And thereby his and his disciples' miraculously expelling of them might be represented of that work that Christ came into the world upon, which was to deliver the souls of men from captivity to Satan, and that it might be an earnest of the future glorious success of his Gospel to that end through the preaching of his apostles and other disciples.

There are two things observable in the manner of the disciples rendering this account of their success:

(1) They speak of it as a thing joyful to them. "Lord, even the devils are subject unto us through thy name." They mention it as [a] thing wonderful that they should be so successful as that the very devils, the powers of darkness, should be made subject to them, that they should be empowered to do such great things as to deliver men from so great a calamity as the possession of devils, through Christ's name, or through commanding them to come out in the name of Christ. It seems to be more than they expected. When Christ sent them he bid them heal the sick, but we have no account that he signified anything to them as that they should be enabled to cast out

devils. When Christ sent out the twelve, Matthew 10:8, he let them know they should cast out devils, but we are not told of his signifying any such thing when he sent out the seventy. So that they should not only heal the sick but be able to cast out devils seems to be greater success than they expected.

(2) It is plain that they relate it as what they supposed would be a pleasing and acceptable account to the Master. "Lord, even the devils are subject unto us through thy name." As much as to say, "Thy mission of us has not been in vain. Thou hast obtained thine end in it. Of such great authority is thy name that the devils cannot stand before it."

3. The third thing we may observe in the words is how Christ receives them and their account, which is visible in the reply he gives: "And he said unto them, I beheld Satan as lightning fall from heaven." By which two things may be perceived:

(1) That he allows and confirms the account they had given. They tell him that the devils are subject {to them through his name}, and he does not call it [into] question, but tells them this as signifying to them that he knows their account to be true.

(2) That he received it. They told it to him as what they supposed would be a relation well pleasing and joyful to him, and his reply shows that it was so indeed. He mentions it to them as a joyful signification of the happy success of his Gospel preached by his ministers that he beheld Satan as lightning [fallen from heaven]; that is, he beheld him swiftly and suddenly cast down, burning and as it were afire, alight with God's wrath, from the dominion and authority that he had usurped in the world, which is represented in the beginning of the twelfth chapter of Revelation as his being cast down from heaven to the earth. {Verses} 7-10, "And there was war in heaven: Michael and his angels fought against the dragon; and the dragon fought and his angels, and prevailed not; neither was their place found any more in heaven. And the great dragon was cast [out], that old serpent, called the Devil, and Satan, which deceiveth the whole world: he was cast out into the earth, [and his angels were cast out with him. And I heard a loud voice saying in heaven, Now is come

salvation, and strength, and the kingdom of our God, and the power of his Christ: for the accuser of our brethren is cast down, which accused them before our God day and night]."

It was now a joyful time with Christ as well as his disciples on this occasion, as further appears by the twenty-first verse. "In that hour Jesus rejoiced in spirit, and said, I thank thee, O Father, Lord of heaven and earth, that thou hast hid these things from the wise and prudent, and hast revealed them unto babes: even so, Father; for so it seemed good in thy sight."

DOCTRINE

When those ministers of the Gospel that have been faithful and successful come to give an account of their success to their Lord that has sent them, Christ and they will rejoice together.

There are three propositions contained in these verses.

Proposition I. That the ministers of the Gospel are sent forth by Jesus Christ. It is Christ that has appointed the order or office of the gospel ministry. The ministerial commission is from [him] who is the Great Shepherd of the sheep. The word which they preach is his Word, and the ordinances which they administer are his ordinances. And they have no authority to minister in holy things but as they derive it from him. Romans 10:15, "And how shall they preach, except they be sent?" And though they be not sent as the twelve apostles and the seventy were, by a command dictated to them immediately from his mouth, yet he has appointed the particular way in which they should [be] called and set apart to the work with a sufficient signification of his will that when his order in this matter is attended, it should be looked upon as being done in his name, and to be done as much by his authority as if done immediately and personally by himself. He has left the commission with rules annexed how it should be transmitted and communicated. And they are to perform all their administrations in his name and act as Christ's messengers, as though God did beseech men by them. And they are to pray them, in Christ's stead, to be reconciled unto God (2 Corinthians 5:20-21). It is Christ that appoints them their work, and they are sent forth into his harvest. And especially are faithful ministers sent by Christ, for they have not only an external call to the work and are regularly set apart to it according to Christ's appointment as to what is visible, but they are called by the Spirit of Christ inwardly influencing them, inclining and disposing them to the work.

They that take up the work and office of the ministry, not that they might serve Christ in it and promote his glory and the salvation of souls, though they may be indispensably obliged to fulfill their ministry when once they have entered upon it yet in some respect [may] be truly said to run before they are sent. But those whose hearts are aright disposed to their work, and this accompanies an external call, may truly be said to be sent by the Spirit of Christ.

Proposition II. There is a time coming when ministers of the Gospel must return to him that sent them, to give him an account of their ministry. As they have been sent forth from him, so they must return again to him. As they have their commission and instructions from him, so they must render an account to him. They are to watch for souls as they that must give an account (Hebrews 13:17).

They that Christ appoints as stewards in his house must give an account of their stewardship. They must give an account to their great Master how they have done the work that he has appointed, what pains they have taken, what diligence they have used, after [what] manner they have handled the Word of God, what care they have taken of the souls of those that are of the flock that he has given them the charge of. And those that have been faithful and successful, when they have finished their embassy, will return to their Lord to give an account [of] what success they have had, as the servants that received the five talents and the two talents declare to their Lord how much they had gained as in the twenty-fifth chapter of Matthew.

Proposition III. When those that have been faithful and successful do thus return to their Lord that sent them and give an account of their success to him, he and they will rejoice together. Here:

First. Jesus Christ will rejoice upon that occasion.[3] We find rejoicing in such things ascribed to God in Scripture. So Deuteronomy 28:63, as "The Lord rejoiced over you to do you good," and Isaiah

62:5, "As the bridegroom rejoiceth over the bride, so shall God rejoice over thee." And in the parable of the prodigal son, [Christ] is represented as rejoicing at the conversion of the sinner, by the great joy and gladness of the father at his son's return. But we must take heed that we do not understand these things in any such sense as implicitly to ascribe to God the mutability and dependence, or any of the imperfections, of finite beings.

But as Christ being a person that exists not only in the divine but human nature, we need not be afraid to say that he will rejoice on occasion of his faithful and successful ministers returning and giving an account of their success, in the most proper sense of such an expression. Christ is represented as rejoicing at the conversion of a sinner in Luke 15:5, "And when he hath found it, he layeth it on his shoulders, rejoicing."

Several reasons may be given why Christ will rejoice in the success of his ministers:

1. He will rejoice in it as in that which is greatly to his own glory and the glory of his Father.[4] The success of the ministers of the Gospel is greatly to the glory of Jesus Christ. The seventy relate their success to Christ in the devils being subject to them through his name as a thing really to Christ's honor. The glory of Christ as the Mediator and Redeemer consists much in the glorious fruits of his redemption, but these appear in the fruits of the labors of his ministers, in their bringing home souls to himself and building them up in holiness. John 17:10, "And all mine are thine, and thine are mine; and I am glorified in them," and 2 Thessalonians 1:11-12, "Wherefore also we pray always for you, that our God would count you worthy of his calling, and fulfill all the good pleasure of his goodness, and the work of faith with power: that the name of our Lord Jesus Christ may be glorified in you."[5]

This he sought more than he did his own ease or freedom from the most amazing sufferings in body and soul, as appears by what he said a little before his last suffering: John 12:27-28, "Now is my soul troubled; and what shall I say? Father, save me from this hour: but for this cause came I unto this hour. Father, glorify thy name." It was very much for this cause that Christ sought his own glory, namely, that he might thereby be under advantage to glorify the Father; as [in] John 17:1, Jesus lifted up his eyes to heaven and said, "Father, glorify thy Son, that thy Son also may glorify thee." And this made Christ the more abundantly to rejoice in his own glory, because therein his Father was glorified. John 13:31, "Now is the Son of man glorified, and God is glorified in him."

But the success of the ministers {of the Gospel} is what tends exceedingly to the glory of God. The people that are converted and brought home to Christ by the preaching of the Gospel are a people that God has especially formed for his glory (Isaiah 43:7).

And to this end they are predestinated and called. Ephesians 1:11-12, "In whom also we have obtained an inheritance, being predestinated according to the purpose of him who worketh all things after the counsel of his own will: that we should be to the praise of his glory."

2. He will rejoice in the success of his ministers, as therein those are saved and made happy that are the objects of his great love. Those in whom the labors of Christ's ministers have success in their saving good are those that Christ has loved with an everlasting love. Jeremiah 31:3, "I have loved thee with an everlasting love: therefore with lovingkindness have I drawn thee." 1 John 4:19, "We love him, because he first loved us." Their names were written on Christ's heart from eternity, as the names of the twelve tribes were graven on the high priest's breastplate.

And they are those that he has loved with a transcendent love, "a love that passeth knowledge" (Ephesians 3:19), a love that was stronger than death. Herein these are redeemed from a most miserable, doleful state and condition that Christ had bowels of pity and compassion to. They are called out of darkness into marvelous light. They are bought out of cruel bondage. Their prison doors are opened, and they are taken out of the horrible pit and miry clay and saved from everlasting destruction. They that were lost are found, and they that were dead are alive again. And those whose welfare was dear to Christ, and that he prized as it were more than his own precious blood, are brought into happy circumstances, are washed and cleansed and sanctified, are become the children of God, and do become excellent, beautiful, and blessed persons; [they] have their souls adorned with the richest ornaments, are possessed of the most invaluable and durable riches; are brought to union with Christ with their whole hearts, to close with him and to love and choose him and follow him; are brought to a right to eternal pleasures and delights, and at last brought into the paradise of God, there to dwell with Christ and to dwell before the throne of God, to have all tears wiped away from their eyes by him, and to be feasted with Christ, and to be led by him to the living fountain of water.

And how joyful must that be to him who has loved them from eternity with so great and strong and dear a love.

3. And lastly, their success is his success. Therein they are not only made happy that he greatly loved and whose happiness he desired, but whose happiness he has greatly sought and labored and most extremely suffered for. The success of faithful ministers' labors is the success of his labors, and of labors in him that were ten thousand times as great and hard as those of the most laborious ministers.

Faithful ministers of the Gospel will labor hard for the salvation of souls, and will deny themselves, and will be willing to undergo hardship as good soldiers of Jesus Christ. They will be of a spirit to spend and be spent for souls. But what are the labors of the most faithful and laborious of the ministers of the Gospel, and what is their self-denial in comparison of the labors and sufferings that Christ has gone through for souls, who has waded through a sea of blood and gone through a furnace of wrath for their salvation? He has purchased them with his own blood. No minister of Christ was expended and was spent for souls as their Master was.

Seeing Christ has done and undergone so much for the salvation and happiness of souls, doubtless he exceedingly rejoices in seeing the travail of his soul. This was the joy that was set before [him], for which he willingly endured the cross and despised {the shame (Hebrews 12:2)}. This success was what God the Father promised him as his reward. Isaiah 53:10-11, "When thou shalt make his soul an offering for sin, he shall see his seed, he shall prolong his days, and the pleasure of the Lord shall prosper in his hand. He shall see of the travail of his soul, and shall be satisfied."

And doubtless it must be greatly to his satisfaction and rejoicing. The height of his joy in his success will in some respect exceed the extremity of his griefs and sufferings that he underwent for it, as is evident because when both were set before him, that outweighed with him, so that he willingly underwent this for the sake of the other.

For these reasons Christ will rejoice when his faithful and successful ministers shall return to him that sent them with an account of their success.

Second. They themselves will then greatly rejoice. They will return to their Lord. They will render up their account with joy as the seventy did.

1. Their love to the Lord that sent them, and for whom they have labored, will cause them to rejoice. The faithful ministers of the Gospel love their Master, and love to him is the principle that governs them in their work, and not filthy lucre or any worldly views. They labor for him and not for themselves. And therefore when they come to him to give him an account of their success, it will be with rejoicing, because their success is that wherein their Lord is glorified and his ends obtained, and because they will be sensible that such an account will be well pleasing and acceptable to him. So the seventy (Luke 10:17) evidently give the relation of their success with joy as well, supposing that it would be an acceptable account to him: "Lord, even the devils are subject unto us through thy name."

Faithful ministers love their Lord above all the world while in their work, but when they come to return to their Lord and shall behold his glory, then will their hearts be drawn forth in love to him in a manner that exceedingly transcends all their exercises of love in this world. And then how joyful will it be to them to consider that they have been the instruments of so advancing the kingdom and glory of their Lord in the world and bringing home those to him that he has purchased with his blood.

2. Their love to the souls that they have been the instruments of

the happiness of will cause them to rejoice. Faithful ministers have a great love to the precious souls of men and therefore willingly labor and spend and are spent for them. They love them before they have been the instruments of their conversion, which makes them so earnestly seek their conversion, and they love them more after they have been the instruments of their conversion, for then they are their children. They have begotten them through the Gospel (1 Corinthians 4:15).

And, which is more, they are then the children of God and the members of the mystical body of Christ. And if this consideration does so endear them to them now, how will their hearts glow with love to them then, when they come to Christ in glory, when their principle of divine love shall be exalted to a glorious height and made perfect in them. And how joyful will it be to consider that they have begotten these and as it were travailed in birth with them, and through their instrumentality they have actually become the children of God and heirs of glory.

3. Their love to themselves will cause them then to rejoice, and that upon three accounts:

(1) Because when the faithful ministers of Christ render an account of their success, [it] will be accepted and allowed by Christ as a seal of their faithfulness. Christ will accept and approve of their account. When they shall declare how much they have gained by their diligent and faithful improvements of the talents their Lord committed to them, they shall be openly commended as good and faithful servants, and the souls they have been the instruments of the salvation of shall be accepted as seals of their ministry. It shall be allowed by their Lord that these are the fruits of their faithfulness. And as Christ gave them to them in this world as the fruits of their labors, so he will, as it were, give them to them hereafter as their crown of rejoicing. And,

(2) They shall then receive a glorious reward for the good they have done in their successful faithfulness. The reward their Lord and Master shall bestow upon such ministers when they return to give him an account shall be exceeding excellent. It is said, Daniel 12:3,

"they that be wise shall shine as the brightness of the firmament; and they that turn many to righteousness as the stars for ever and ever." Christ will then not only approve them and say, "Well done, thou good and faithful servant," but he will moreover say, "Enter into the joy of thy Lord" [Matthew 25:21]. And this will be abundant cause for them to rejoice.

(3) The people who have [been] awakened.

4. Christ and they with him not only shall rejoice, but shall rejoice together as the seventy and Christ did, and as we are expressly told Christ and faithful and successful ministers will, in John 4:35-36: "Say not ye, There are yet four months, and then cometh harvest? behold, I say unto you, Lift up your eyes, and look on the fields; for they are white already to harvest. And he that reapeth receiveth wages, and gathereth fruit unto life eternal: that both he that soweth and he that reapeth may rejoice together."

Christ seems to be the person that is here meant by him that soweth, and his ministers are those that reap. Gospel ministers are only as it were sent forth to reap the fruit of his labors. They do not save men, but are only sent forth to bring in those that he has saved. It is Christ that has, as it were, plowed and sowed the field and by his own great labors and sufferings laid all the foundations of their salvation. And ministers have nothing to do but to reap and gather in the harvest as it is represented in our context, verse 2: the harvest is plenteous, "but the laborers are few: pray ye therefore the Lord of the harvest, that he would send forth laborers into his harvest." Christ in his lifetime sowed the seed, but it was the disciples after his ascension that reaped the harvest, which is what Christ seems to refer to in the thirty-seventh verse. And herein is that saying true, one soweth and another reapeth. He that sows is the owner of the field and Lord of the harvest; ministers are laborers—indeed, they are servants.

By Christ and their rejoicing together seems to be signified something more than merely then that Christ and they both shall rejoice. [There] is held forth a communion between Christ and them in each other's joy, and particularly it implies the following things:

(1) It implies that when they shall then rejoice, they shall be together as friends. This communion in their joy implies a union. Ministers that have not been faithful must return to him that sent them as their judge to give an account. But Christ's faithful ministers shall return to him after they have done their work and meet him as dear friends meet after long absence. They shall come as disciples to a dear Lord and as children to a Father, as the seventy did. Christ and they will rejoice together on this occasion as friends. Thus we read that when the good shepherd had found his lost sheep, he is said to call together his friends and neighbors saying, "Rejoice with me; for I have found {my sheep which was lost," Luke 15:6}.

Gospel ministers that have been the instruments of the rescuing of the lost sheep shall especially be some of those friends that will be called to rejoice with the Chief Shepherd.

(2) Another thing implied is that they shall rejoice as jointly interested and mutually concerned in this affair. He that sows and he that reaps are both interested in the same harvest, though the Lord of the harvest be primarily so. The success of his labors is the success of their labors, travail, and blood. The Great Shepherd and the under-shepherds are jointly concerned, and their success is his success, and their crown his crown. They have jointly acted in the affair. Their Lord and Master is he that has given them grace to be faithful, and it is he that has given them success. The work that has been done has been his work, and they have been concerned only as instruments in his hand. His faithful ministers have wrought for him in that work that they have been successful in, and he has also wrought for them, otherwise they never could have been successful. Their faithful labors have been out of love to Christ, and their success has been an instance of Christ's great love to them.

They will rejoice together as those that are, as it were, the occasions of each other's joy. Christ will rejoice on occasion of their success and the joyful account they give him of it. And they will rejoice in the great mercy they have received from him whereby they have been enabled to be faithful and successful.

(3) Another thing implied is that their joy shall be mutually man-

ifested. So it was when the seventy returned. They manifest their joy to their Master by their manner of speaking to him when they give him an account of their success. And he manifests his joy to them in the reply he makes to them.

So when faithful and successful ministers return to their Lord with an account of their success, they will show [their joy] to their Lord, and they shall see that their Lord also rejoices.

(4) And lastly, they shall rejoice in each other's joy. Their rejoicing together implies that their joy shall not only be mutually manifested, but mutually communicated.

Thus it was when the seventy returned. They evidently rejoiced at the thoughts of the acceptableness of the relation they had to give to Christ, and how pleasing it would be to him. On the other hand, Christ rejoiced in their gladness. He is well pleased in the joy of his dear disciples. Thus Christ's faithful ministers shall enter into the joy of their Lord, and his joy shall be fulfilled in themselves, agreeable to John 17:13. And they shall mutually partake in each other's rejoicing. And they shall sup with him, and he with [them] and they with him. And they shall, as it were, drink new wine with him in his heavenly Father's kingdom.

APPLICATION

In a few inferences:

Inference I. Hence we may learn what a blessed work the work of the gospel ministry [is]. What an excellent and honorable employment must that be which is concerned about that which is so great and glorious in its end and issues as the joint and mutual gladness of the laborers and of him that is the Great Head of the church and the Lord of angels.

Any employment is justly looked upon [as] excellent and honorable according as the work done is important, excellent, and happy. But what employment is there that the children of men are employed in wherein the effect or success or work done is so glorious and blessed?

This is a most excellent work, on account of the blessed issue of the success of the labors of those that are faithful in it to themselves—what honor and happiness does it bring them to, in bringing of them to rejoice in glory with Jesus Christ. There is no employment that the children of men are employed in wherein they have such opportunity to lay a foundation for their own blessedness. Faithfulness in serving God in any calling will be crowned with glorious rewards, but there seem to be promises of distinguished and peculiar honors and joys to a faithfulness in this work, and especially a successful faithfulness as in that forementioned place in Daniel 12:3 and other places. And this employment may well be looked on as a yet more excellent and honorable employment on the account of the joy that the success of it occasions to Christ. The very business of those that are called to this employment is to do that in which Christ exceedingly rejoices.

Surely that must be great and excellent indeed that the Lord of angels and men takes such notice of and so rejoices in. Is not that honorable to such little, inferior creatures as we to be employed to do that which, when done, rejoices the heart of the Son of God?

The work of ministers is to rescue lost souls and bring them to eternal happiness, which is the work that Christ himself came into the world upon and shed his blood for. It is to be the instruments of Christ's success in the work of redemption, which God looks on and speaks of as the most glorious of all his works.

The success of this work was the joy and crown that Christ had set before [him], for which he endured the cross and despised the shame. And what honor is that that is conferred on the children of men, that they should be employed in putting this crown of joy upon Christ's head, in that they are the instruments of bringing to pass the work of conversion which is the marriage between Christ and his spouse. The day of their conversion is the day of Christ's espousals and the day of the gladness of his heart. It is thought to have been a custom among the Israelites that on the wedding day the mother of the bridegroom put a crown upon his head, to be a crown of joy and rejoicing, which is mystically applied to Christ in Canticles 3:11: "Go forth, O ye daughters of Zion, and behold king

Solomon with the crown wherewith his mother crowned him in the day of his espousals, and in the day of the gladness of his heart." By King Solomon is doubtless meant Christ, and by his mother and his bride both is meant the church. But by his mother seems especially to be meant the church as holding forth the Word of Christ and administering his ordinances, whereby souls are converted and as it were brought forth and brought to a spiritual marriage with Christ. And therefore the ministers of the Gospel seem especially to be intended by his mother, for they travail in birth with souls till Christ is formed in them (Galatians 4:19). Christ said of his disciples, "They are my brother and sister and mother" {Matthew 12:49}. These, therefore, when they are the instruments of converting souls and their espousal to Christ, do as it were put a crown of gladness on Christ's head. And what an honor is thus put upon worms of the dust. Every time that a faithful minister is an instrument of the conversion of any person, it brings a soul to espousals with Christ and occasions gladness in his heart and adds a jewel to his crown of rejoicing. And hereafter when they come to give an account to their Lord of their success, they shall then behold this crown of joy which they have set on Christ's head, and Christ will at the same [time] give the same jewels to them to be their own crowns of rejoicing. And thus they shall have communion in the same crown of joy, which shows the exceeding blessedness of this work. Though the work of the ministry be not ordinarily a work of such temporal advantage in this land as in some other places, nor as it has formerly been in this land, yet what cause have those that are employed in it and are faithful in it and in a measure successful to rejoice in it on account of these unspeakable spiritual and eternal honors and blessings that Christ has annexed to it.

The issue of the work, when faithfully attended and succeeded, is on all accounts joyful. It not only occasions joy to the laborers in it and joy to Christ, but what happiness and glory is the fruit of it to those on whom it is successful. Their souls are saved from death and brought to eternal joy and glory. And not only so, but it occasions joy to all heaven, for "there is joy in the presence of the angels of God over one sinner that repenteth" (Luke 15:10). The joy of Christ will be the joy of all heaven. All those numerous host rejoice when he rejoices.

Inference II. What motive is here to ministers of the Gospel to be faithful and earnestly to seek to be successful in this great and excellent work. What has been said shows how blessed such ministers [are], let their circumstances in this world be what they will. Here,

First. Let us who are employed or are about to be employed in this work consider how blessed a day that day will [be] to us, wherein we return to our Lord to give an account, if we have been faithful and successful. Let us consider how it will be when we die, which we shortly must. And let us consider how it will be at the day of judgment, when we see those persons standing with us at Christ's right hand, shining in glory, that we have been the instruments of the conversion and salvation of, and of their building up in holiness and being made meet for his glory. Then they will be a crown of rejoicing to us. 1 Thessalonians 2:19-20, "For what is our hope, or joy, or crown of rejoicing? Are not even ye in the presence of our Lord Jesus Christ at his coming? Ye are our glory and joy." When we shall have it to say to our Lord, with rejoicing, "Lord, these are the souls that through thy grace we have travailed in birth with, these are the fruits of those diligent and faithful labors thou hast assisted us [in]"; and when we shall see manifestations of joy in our Lord and Master on this occasion, and he shall allow and confirm our account; and when he shall in reward for it crown us with a crown of rejoicing and set us in distinguished glory and cause us to shine as the brightness of the firmament; and when we shall be admitted into fellowship and intimate conversation with our Lord and relate to him our labors and self-denial through his grace and the blessed success we had in one instance and another; we know not after what particular manner the saints in glory shall converse with Christ, but we have reason to conclude from the Word of God that they shall be admitted as friends to converse freely with him, no less freely than the disciples on earth did. And what joyful conversation will this be between Christ and his faithful and successful ministers of their labors and success, when the souls in whom their success is visible [shall] be present in glory with [them], and all are rejoicing together.

Second. Let it be considered that if we are faithful, though we have but little success, we shall [not] fail of a glorious reward. Though there be a distinguished crown for a successful faithfulness, ministers' faithfulness has in itself no sufficiency or efficacy to obtain success. Paul may plant, "Apollos watered; but God gave the increase" [1 Corinthians 3:6]. When therefore the want of success has not been for want of sincere endeavors and earnest diligence, their want of success will not be an occasion of their failing of a reward.

Third. How dreadful will our case be when we come to give an account to our Lord if we have been unfaithful; if when we have been betrusted with the care of the precious souls of men and have been called to so honorable a work, if we have neglected our work or done it slightly and have regarded only or chiefly our worldly concerns, that we might live splendidly and hoard up for our posterity. When we shall see those precious souls that were committed to our care lost through our neglect and standing at the left hand of the Judge in horrid amazement, and they shall rise up in judgment against us and shall declare how we neglected their souls, in such a case their blood will be required at our hands, as we are taught, Ezekiel 3:18. Instead of meeting our Lord with joy, with what dreadful horror shall we behold his face, in which there will be no tokens of rejoicing at the relations we have to give him, but tokens of wrath and fearful indignation, ready to lower us into distinguished torment and misery. For though the work of the ministry be so honorable and blessed a work in itself, it is a most dangerous employment to the unfaithful and those that undertake it and attend only for filthy lucre. And as faithful ministers shall be distinguished in glory, so perhaps none will be so distinguished in misery as unfaithful ministers. And though they may have had some success, let it be more or less, they shall have no reward for it if it has not been through their faithful endeavors.

Fourth. Let us consider that faithfulness is the way to success. Though it be true that a minister may be faithful and yet be in a great measure unsuccessful and have cause to complain—Isaiah 49:4, "I have labored in vain, I have spent [my strength for nought, and in vain]"—yet this is the way to success, and God usually blessed the labors of his faithful ministers in a greater or lesser degree. Jeremiah 23:22, "if they had stood in my counsel, and had caused my people to hear my words, then they should have turned them from their evil way, and from the evil of their doings." If we love our work and rejoice in it, and earnestly wish and seek and strive for success, and have hearts prepared to rejoice in it now, Christ probably will give us the honor and happiness of rejoicing with him in our success hereafter. But,

Inference III. And lastly, hence we may learn what obligations a people are under to do all that lies in their power to promote their minister's success, by encouraging him in his work, enabling of him to attend it without distraction and with good advantage by a sufficient maintenance; by taking care of his temporal affairs and supplying him with those things that are necessary, so that he may be at leisure and in a capacity to attend and give himself wholly to that great work to which he is called; and by loving their minister and manifesting a kind spirit to him, being ready on all occasions to help him and show him kindness, and to strengthen and not weaken his hands in prayers for him; in being ready to hearken to his counsel and to submit to him in his work. It depends much on a people that their minister should attain this crown of joy that we have been speaking of, and in preventing of it they prevent their own joy and happiness. Hebrews 13:17, "Obey them that have the rule over you, and submit yourselves: for they watch for your souls, as they that must give account, that they may do it with joy, and not with grief: for that is unprofitable for you." From what has been said, we learn that they herein do not only promote their minister's joy, but they are occasions of joy to Jesus Christ by these things. And whose joy and happiness do they promote more than their own, for their minister's success consists in their salvation and eternal happiness? People that keep their minister low in the world and oppose him in his work and weaken his hands do but fight against their own souls and undermine their own everlasting welfare.

NOTES

1   Lucius R. Paige, *The History of Hardwick, Massachusetts. With a Genealogical Register* (Boston: Houghton, Mifflin and Company, 1883), 176.

2   Edwards deleted with a vertical line: "The joy with which their hearts were affected appears both in its being expressly said that they returned with joy, but their joy appears in what they say to their Lord and the manner of their speaking. But this brings to observe."

3   Edwards deleted with a diagonal line: "Rejoicing is to be attributed in one sense to Christ as God and in another sense as man. Rejoicing in the success of the faithful ministers of the gospel must not be ascribed to Christ as God in any sense inconsistent with the divine immutability and absolute independence but yet."

4   Edwards deleted with a vertical line: "The Son of God as he is in the bosom of the Father so he has an infinite love to him. There was a mutual infinite love and delight between the Father and the Son from all eternity. Proverbs 8:30, 'I was daily his delight.' And none ever sought the glory of God the Father as Christ has done. Nor ever has any done and gone through so much for it as he has. He has done more to glorify his Father than all the servants and angels in heaven and on earth have done."

5   Edwards deleted with a vertical line: "The souls that are brought hence to Christ and built up in him to his heavenly kingdom, Christ looks upon as being as it were a glorious ornament and crown to him, their Redeemer and Head. Zechariah 9:16, 'And the Lord their God shall save them in that day as the flock of his people: for they shall be as the stones of a crown, lifted up as an ensign upon his land.' Herein consisted great part of that glory that God the Father promised the Son as the crown of redemption as a reward for his labors and sufferings in the work of redemption."

5

EDITORS' INTRODUCTION

DEACONS TO CARE FOR THE BODY, MINISTERS FOR THE SOUL

Edwards preached this sermon in August 1739, at a service in which his Northampton church ordained some of their members as deacons. Like other Congregationalists of his day, Edwards believed Christ had instituted two offices to govern the church, the office of deacon and the office of pastor or elder or "bishop," as Edwards prefers to call it in this sermon. In it he differentiates the duties of the two. Although Edwards preached this for a deacon ordination, he used the opportunity to teach as much about the duties of ministers as about the duties of deacons.

In the apostolic era Christ appointed such "extraordinary" officers as apostles and prophets, Edwards said, but Christ ordained that at all other times the church's ordinary officers should consist of bishops and deacons. Christ appointed bishops to care for the needs of the soul and deacons to care for the needs of the body. Edwards saw in this divine arrangement evidence of the tenderness and faithfulness of Christ toward his church in making provision thus for bodily and spiritual needs.

Edwards did not specify the duties of each office, but rather explained the different character and aim of each. All of Christ's officers are appointed to do good to the church under their care, he said. For deacons, to do good meant "to satisfy the church's poor with bread," and to do so equitably and efficiently. For ministers, to do good to the church meant being the "instruments of their souls' salvation."

Edwards's treatment of church government and its two officers represents a traditional Congregational approach. It does not vary in these areas from the Cambridge Platform, the form of church government agreed upon by Massachusetts's clergy in 1648. Edwards did not, however, discuss the office of ruling elder, a "lay" minister whose duties included governing the church and administering its spiritual matters but excluded preaching and teaching and administering the sacraments. Early New England churches ordained ruling elders, but by Edwards's time the churches generally neglected to do so.

The manuscript, held by the Beinecke Rare Book and Manuscript Library, Yale University, consists of thirteen duodecimo leaves. At the top of the first page, Edwards wrote, "On occasion of the ordination of the deacons Aug[ust] 19, 1739."

Deacons to Care for
the Body, Ministers
for the Soul

ROMANS 12:4-8

For as we have many members in one body, and all members have not the same office: so we, being many, are one body in Christ, and every one members one of another. Having then gifts differing according to the grace that is given to us, whether prophecy, let us prophesy according to the proportion of faith; or ministry, let us wait on our ministering: or he that teacheth, on teaching; or he that exhorteth, on exhortation: he that giveth, let him do it with simplicity; he that ruleth, with diligence; he that showeth mercy, with cheerfulness.

In the words we may observe three things:

1. We observe what is the theme of the apostle's discourse in these verses, namely, the different offices there are in the church of Christ, as in the first of these verses: ["For as we have many members in one body, and all members have not the same office"]. So in the sixth [through eighth] verse[s], he speaks of the different gifts that are exercised in the church in those different offices.

2. Here is an account of the business belonging to these several

offices rehearsed in a variety of expressions: prophesying, teaching, exhorting, ruling, ministering, giving, showing mercy.

Concerning these businesses that the apostle speaks of in this place, as belonging to the different offices that are in the church, we may observe two things:

(1) That they all concern the welfare of the church, as it is in that to which the apostle compares it, namely, the natural body. Different members of the body have different offices, but the office of every member is [in] some way to subserve to the benefit of the body. So it is in the body of Christ; the different offices that are in it respect the benefit of the body, or of the church. The business that belongs to each officer in the society is to do good to the society, though the business of one office is to do good to the society in one respect, and another in another.

Thus, to prophesy, to teach, to exhort, and to rule is to do good to those that are taught, exhorted, and ruled. So to minister, give, and show mercy is still another way to do good to the members of the body.[1]

(2) It may be observed that all those businesses of officers in the church that are here mentioned are of two sorts. Some of them respect the souls of men and some their bodies. They all are to do good to the members of the society in which they are officers, but there are two ways of doing good to the society. One is to do good to their souls, and another is to do good to their bodies.

And it is observable that all the businesses here mentioned are one or the other of these. Prophesying, teaching, exhorting, and ruling all respect the souls of men. They are so many different ways of officers doing good to the souls of the society. But the other things mentioned—ministering, giving, and showing mercy—especially respect the good of their bodies.

So that there are two sorts of work of a distinct kind that the apostle mentions when he reckons up the kinds of work that belong to the different offices in the church. One is to do good to the souls, and the other is to do good to the bodies of men.

And it is observable that all these businesses here mentioned that concern men's souls belong to the office of elders or bishops—prophesying, teaching, exhorting, and ruling. The other therefore, namely, ministering, giving, showing mercy, that concerns the bodies of men, belongs to some other office Christ has appointed in his church. All three expressions—ministering, giving, and showing mercy—are only a diversity expressing the same thing. By ministering, as the word used in the New Testament is most commonly meant, [is] meant giving or communicating of our goods to others. So the apostle Paul when he was going to Jerusalem to carry the contributions of other churches to the poor saints there says, Romans 15:25, "But now I go to Jerusalem to minister to the saints." So in 2 Corinthians 8:4, speaking of the same contribution, he says, "Praying us with much intreaty that we would receive the gift, and take upon us the fellowship of ministering to the saints." So when he exhorts the Corinthians to the same contribution, he says, 9:1, "For as touching the ministering to the saints, it is needless that I write unto you." So when the apostle commends the Christian Hebrews for their charity to the saints, he says, Hebrews 6:10, "For God is not unrighteous to forget your work and labor of love, which ye have showed towards his name, in that ye have ministered to the saints, and do minister." And so in innumerable other places that might be mentioned.

And therefore Mr. [Matthew] Henry, in his *Annotations*, says that when the apostle says in the text, "or ministry, let us wait on our ministering," he has respect to the office of deacons, as that is the general opinion of expositors and divines.[2]

The word that is translated "deacons" is in the original *diakonoi*. The signification of the word is "they that minister." The name is taken from their business, which is to minister to the saints. This is the business spoken of here: "or ministry, let us wait in our ministering." The word *ministry* in the text in the original is *diakonia* or deaconship. Whence Mr. Henry argues that the office of a deacon is meant in the text. What this ministering is, is plainly signified in the following expression of "giving and showing mercy."

3. [The third] thing that is observable in the words is the counsel

the apostle gives to the different officers of the church to execute the
business of their offices well, and to the church to perform well the
business they performed by their offices. Bishops or elders were to
wait on their teaching, exhorting, and ruling, and the deacons on
their ministering, giving, and showing mercy.

"Or ministry, let us wait on our ministering; [. . .] he that
giveth, let him do it with simplicity; he that ruleth, with diligence;
he that showeth mercy, with cheerfulness." Which may be looked
upon as an exhortation both to those officers of the church whose
business it was to take care [of] and minister to the saints, that
should take the care and burden of their office and serve as cheerfully as a work of mercy and charity and do it with simplicity and
faithfulness; and also to the church with respect to the work that
they did by these offices, their showing mercy by them, that they
should do it cheerfully.

DOCTRINE

*The officers that Christ has appointed in his church do respect either the
souls or bodies of men.*

As it was observed, the business of all officers in the church was
[in] some way to do good to the members of the society in which they
were officers, and it is in one or the other of these ways: either to do
good to their souls or to their bodies.

In treating of this I would,

I. Observe what are the different offices that Christ has appointed
in his church, and,

II. That the work of these offices respects either the souls or bodies of men.

I. Observe what are the offices {that Christ has appointed in his
church}. Offices are either extraordinary or ordinary.

First. There have been extraordinary offices that Christ {has
appointed in his church}. By extraordinary offices is meant such
offices as are founded on an extraordinary and immediate call of
God, and in the exercises of which the officers depended on extraordinary and miraculous gifts of the Holy Ghost. So the prophets of

old were extraordinary officers. So were the apostles and evangelists, and those that spoke with tongues and had gifts of healing and other miraculous gifts that we read of in the New Testament. These extraordinary officers were of temporary continuance because, they depending on miraculous gifts of the Holy Ghost, when those miraculous gifts cease, these extraordinary offices must of course cease.

Second. There are ordinary officers that Christ has appointed in his church. These are two, namely, bishops and deacons. We have an account of these two in the first Christian church that was set up after Christ's resurrection, namely, the church of Jerusalem, from whence all other Christian churches are derived, and [it] is set forth as a pattern to all other Christian churches in its constitution. There were then teaching and ruling officers, the apostles and other ministers, and there was the office of deacons first set up as we have an account in the sixth chapter of Acts. So when the apostle mentions the stated officers of the church in the first verse of his epistle to the Philippians, he mentions these two, bishops and deacons.

And when the apostle Paul gives directions to Timothy concerning the qualifications of officers in the church, he mentions but these two, namely, bishops and deacons, in the First Epistle to Timothy, third chapter. And these two offices, bishop and deacon, by the universal consent of divines and of all Christian churches, are both perpetual and constantly to be upheld in the church to the end of the world. But I hasten,

II. To show that the work of these different offices Christ has appointed in his church respects either the souls or bodies of men. Hence,

First. So it was when there were extraordinary offices in the church of Christ, such as apostles and gifts of tongues and gifts of healing and the like. Some of these extraordinary gifts related immediately to the good of men's souls; such was the gift of prophecy and the gift of tongues and others. Other of these gifts related more immediately to the good of men's bodies; such were gifts of healing.

There were in those times of extraordinary officers some inspired by God with extraordinary gifts to teach and enlighten men's minds and to relieve and deliver men's souls. And others [who] had extraordinary gifts were extraordinarily enabled to show mercy to men's bodies and deliver them from their calamities and miseries. They labored under the same things that Christ did when he was on earth, who relieved men's bodies under all manner of sickness and disease and wounds and torments they labored under. They were enabled to show mercy to men's bodies by restoring the sick, curing the lame and maimed, easing men's pains, loosing the tongue of the dumb, unstopping the ears of the deaf, opening the eyes {of the blind}, and delivering them from all manner of calamities their bodies labored under.

Second. So it is in the ordinary offices that Christ has appointed in his church, namely, these two of bishops and deacons. The former respects the souls of men, and the latter their bodies. And because these two are the offices that we are especially concerned to understand the nature [of], being the standing ordinary offices of Christ's church that continue to this day and must continue to the end of the world, I will therefore be a little more particular in explaining the nature of them and will then give the reasons of the doctrine. And here I would:

1. Show wherein these two offices of bishops and deacons agree; and,

2. Wherein they differ.

1. I will show wherein these two sorts of officers agree.

(1) They are both of them overseers and watchmen in the church of God. The business of bishops or elders is to take the oversight of the church of God for their good, to be watchmen, to observe the circumstances and needs of the flock, that they may be supplied; and so it is with deacons also.

(2) They are both stewards in the house of God. The business of both is alike in that they are stewards to take care to supply the wants of Christ's family. The business [of] both is to feed God's people. The

business of both is to see to it that everyone has his portion of meat in due season.

2. But with regard to that wherein they differ, the great difference lies in this, that one relates to the souls of God's people, and the other to their bodies. Bishops are overseers and wat[chmen] of the flock with respect to their souls. Deacons are overseers with respect to their bodies. Bishops are to have a watchful eye on the state of the whole flock, to observe the circumstances of their souls, that they may adapt spiritual supplies to their particular necessities. So deacons are to have a watchful eye on the state of the whole flock also, to take notice of the circumstances of their bodies, to observe who are under straits and in necessities, that their necessities may be supplied. Bishops are stewards of the household, that every one may have his portion of meat in due season in spiritual respects. Deacons are stewards in the same household, that everyone that is in necessity and is a proper object of charity may be relieved and may have his portion of meat in due season, as appears by the first occasion of the institution of the office of deacons in the sixth chapter of Acts, which was the poor being neglected.

As it is in the houses of earthly princes—they keep two sorts of stewards in their families; they have their chaplains and tutors that are to take the care of the instruction of the family and are to pray with [them] and take care of their souls and are a kind of spiritual stewards; and then besides, they have their stewards who are to take care for the outward supply of the family—so it is in the family of Christ, the King of kings. This business, which was the first occasion of the institution of this office, is the most essential business of the office. Though there be other businesses also that it is proper for deacons to do: as to take care of the provision of the Lord's Table, and also to be ready to assist those that are in the pastoral office in what relates to their outward support, so far as the present circumstances of the church of Christ require it; for there are many things they may occasionally do whereby the minister may be much helped, and that office supported and encouraged, though their main support does not come through their hands as formerly it did. Though the end of committing the church flock into the hands of the deacons was especially to supply the poor, as the Scripture is plain, yet as they had the whole flock in their hands, so doubtless they disposed of it to all those uses for which the church had need of it. And so we may argue that they supplied the Table of the Lord and of their pastors, but that which was the special occasion of the institution is doubtless the most essential business.

It was a thing established by the church of God from the very beginning that a part of the substance of God's visible people should be brought as an offering to the Lord. So it was in the family of Adam. This was a duty that he trained up his two sons, Cain and Abel, in. What they did was not only in compliance with the institution of families, but what they had been trained up as their duty, to offer to God a part of their substance. Cain brought of the fruit of the ground an offering to the Lord, doing his duty therein as the tiller of it—though he did not do it with a right spirit. And it has always been a thing established from the beginning of the world that God's visible people should offer a part of their substance to God as part of their public service of God in his church. When Cain and Abel are said to have brought their offering to the Lord, thereby is doubtless meant that they brought their offerings either to Adam's altar or the place where Adam's family was wont to meet with God and worship God.

But I now proceed to the reasons of the doctrine, or the reasons why there should be these two sorts of officers appointed in the church, one to take [care] of the souls, and the other the bodies, of his people.

(1) This answers to the two constituent parts of man's nature, of which Christ is the Savior. Men differ from angels in this, that whereas they are pure spirits, man consists of a twofold substance, namely, a spiritual substance, which is his soul, and a material substance, which is his body. When man fell, he ruined both body and soul, and Christ is the Redeemer of both and has taken both under his care. Both are redeemed by Christ, and therefore both are to be

given to Christ as being both his. 1 Corinthians 6:19-20, "What? know ye not that your body is the temple [of the Holy Ghost which is in you, which ye have of God,] and ye are not your own? For ye are bought with a price: therefore glorify God in your body, and in your spirit, which are his." Not only the souls but the bodies of Christians are said to be the temples of the Holy Ghost, and their bodies, as well as souls, are members of Christ. 1 Corinthians 6:15, "Know ye not that your bodies are the members of Christ?" Agreeable to this, Christ has appointed two sorts of officers in his church, that both these might be well taken care of, one to take care of the bodies, and the other of the souls of his people.

(2) This is agreeable to the two sorts of needs of his people. They consisting of these two parts, their needs are of two kinds. They be not only needs of soul but of body. Matthew 6:8, "Your heavenly Father knoweth that ye have need of these things." And as a Father cares for the supply of all the needs of his children, so it is with the heavenly Father of the church. Philippians 4:19, "But my God shall supply all your need according to his riches in glory by Christ Jesus."

(3) Herein the stated services of God's house are agreeable to the two sorts of commands that he has given to his people, namely, the commands of the first and second table.

As there are two kinds of commands, one sort more immediately respecting our duty to God, and the other more immediately respecting our duty to man, so God has appointed two sorts of services to be attended [to] in his house. The one, that sort that consists in the immediate worship of God in performance of the duties of the first table. The commands of the first table relate to the worship of God, and therefore God has appointed one kind of officer for the performance of those sort of services in his house, namely, the office of a bishop. All those services of God's house wherein the immediate worship of God consists are to be performed by the minister.

But then, as here, is another sort of commands, the commands of the second table, which respect the good of our neighbor. The principal duty of which is charity to our neighbor (yea, love or charity to our neighbor is the sum of the duties of the second table). And therefore God has also appointed another sort of service constantly to be kept up in his house, answerable to this second sort of commands, namely, a service of charity and mercy, and so has appointed a second sort of officers to attend these services. It is the will of God that those services that consist in duties of the second table, duties of charity to our neighbor, should statedly be upheld in the Christian church, as well as duties of the first table consisting in the worship of God. And when this fails, [a] great part of the appointed service of God's house fails, and the business of one of these two sorts of officers Christ has appointed in his church ceases.

Mercy is a service of the Christian church to be upheld statedly in it, as sacrifice was in the church of the Jews. Sacrifice has ceased. That was a very chargeable sort of worship in the church of the Jews, but God has appointed mercy in the Christian church in the room of it, that they may bring their offerings to God in another way. For what is given to the poor is offered to God as much as the sacrifices were. For he that gives to the poor lends to the Lord.

And God has declared that this is a more acceptable way of making offerings to God than sacrifices. And therefore he has said that he will have mercy and not sacrifice, Matthew 9:13. Now in these gospel days, he has abolished the first that he might establish the second.

And the apostle speaks of what is given to the poor in the Christian church as contrary to sacrifices. Hebrews 13:16, "But to do good and to communicate forget not: for with such sacrifices God is well pleased." God has ordered that the charge which the church was wont to be at of old in sacrifices should now in the Christian church be turned another way, namely, to acts [of] mercy, and has appointed a certain kind of officers to this end.

And so now there are services of both the first and second table of the Law appointed in the church, and officers to attend both.

(4) This is agreeable to the two sorts of work that Christ did when he was personally present with his church on earth, which was to instruct the souls and show mercy to the bodies of men. The work of

Christ during his own ministry on earth was to show mercy to men. And this consisted in these two things: *[1.]* In showing mercy to their souls by preaching the Gospel and setting it home for their spiritual good, and accordingly he went about teaching and preaching; and *[2.]* the other work that he abounded in was in showing mercy to men's bodies under their outward miseries, healing all manner of sickness, feeding the hungry.

And now he is gone to heaven; yet he has taken care that the same two sorts of work should be continued in his church and has therefore appointed officers to that end. In the primitive times, while extraordinary gifts were continued, both these kinds of works, namely, teaching men's souls and showing mercy to their bodies, were continued in the same extraordinary way in which Christ himself performed them, namely, by supplies immediately from heaven. But since [then] they are continued in the ordinary way of supplying men's souls out of the written Word of God and helping their bodies in the use of ordinary means and supplies of life.

(5) This is agreeable to the two sorts of promises of the covenant of grace, namely, the things of this life and that which is to come. Christ's promises to his church are of these two kinds. 1 Timothy 4:8, "For bodily exercise profiteth little: but godliness is profitable to all things, having the promise of the life that now is, and of that which is to come."

So we find both these kinds of promises implied. Matthew 6:33, "Seek ye first the kingdom of God, and his righteousness; and all other things shall be added unto you."

Now, it is an instance of Christ's faithfulness of these promises that he has taken such special care that both should be fulfilled that when he ascended into heaven he appointed a kind of officers for both these ends, that both these promises might be fulfilled, not only by his own sovereign providence, but also in a way of the appointed institutions of his house. And so he appointed one officer to be the instrument of fulfilling one, and another to be the instrument of fulfilling the other kind of promises.

APPLICATION

I. Hence we may see the excellent wisdom of Christ in the constitution of his church. We may see how agreeable this constitution [is] to our nature, that consists of body and soul, and how agreeable it is to his commands that are of two kinds, relating to the worship of God and to the good of our neighbors; how agreeable to the nature of his redemption which respects body and soul; how agreeable to the nature of the covenant of grace, which contains promises; how agreeable to his own example, that when he was on earth [he] filled up his time with these two sorts of work. The more we consider the Christian constitution in all the parts of it, the more shall we see cause to admire that wonderful agreement and harmony there is between one part and another of it, how commands, promises, examples, and offices and officers all agree together as the several parts of a skillful frame, in which every part is fitly joined together and compacted, and one thing beautifully answers another.

By this we may see how the same wisdom appears in the constitution of the mystical body of Christ that appears in the frame of the natural body. In the natural body there are members of various sorts provided to answer the various necessities of the body. There are eyes provided to guide and direct the body, and there are hands to supply the body, to feed it, and to help the other members when wounded or in a suffering state. So it is in the body of Christ. The office of ministers fitly answers to the office of the eye that guides and directs the body. The office of a deacon seems well to answer the office of the hand in the natural body, that feeds it and helps its suffering members.

That there should be an office in the Christian church to take care that the duty of charity may be exercised and its fruits bestowed to the best advantage, as well as an office to teach men's souls, shows how wisely Christ has constituted his church in a harmonious agreement with the nature of the gospel dispensation that we live under, that is so much a dispensation of love, and in which the duty of charity is so much insisted on. When the psalmist is speaking of the glory of that dispensation that should be in the gospel times, when God should cause the horn of David to bud forth and should cause his seed to sit on his throne forever, in Psalm 132, these two things are mentioned together as part of the glory of this gospel dispensation—namely, that God should satisfy the church's poor with bread, and that he should clothe his priests with salvation, verses 15-16, agreeable to the design of these two offices that God has appointed under this dispensation: the office of deacons, which is to satisfy the church's poor with bread, and the office of the priests or ministers, which is to be the instruments of their souls' salvation.

And God's appointing these two offices in the Christian church is a remarkable fulfillment of this prophecy, for there are two offices appointed for these very ends: one office appointed to satisfy her poor with bread, and another for her spiritual and eternal salvation. The success of one, namely, the deacons, is expressed in the church's poor being satisfied with bread, and the success of the other, namely, her priests, is expressed by their being clothed with salvation.

How agreeable is this to the end for which Christ came into the world, which was an errand of mercy, seeing that the duty is so much insisted on by Christ, even in his dying charge to his disciples when he told them that this was his command, his command by way of aspeaking that they should love one another. And {he} told them that this should be the distinguishing duty of the Christian church, that all men should know that they were his disciples by this, that they love one another, John 13:34-35.

I say, seeing it is thus, how wisely has Christ done in appointing an order of men an opportunity to take care of this business for the better management of this great and distinguishing Christian duty.

The wisdom of Christ appears in that he has not left it only at the discretion of every single person, but in appointing some to oversee the business, that the business may be more equally and effectually done, that some may not be neglected while others are overloaded, but that all may have their portion of meat in due season.

How wisely has Christ appointed this way of his church expending charge in his service, instead of the charge they used to be at in sacrificing, and in declaring that he will have mercy and not sacrifice. II. Hence we may see the mercy and tenderness and faithfulness of Christ towards his church. The church is called the family of God (Ephesians 3:15) and the household of God (Ephesians 2:19), and believers are called Christ's children (Hebrews 2:13). He calls them his little children (John 13:33).

By this it appears that Christ deals with his church as a father, as a merciful and tender father that is concerned for the welfare of his family in body and soul and pities them under all straits and difficulties and necessity, and when they want food will supply them and take care that all the household have their portion of meat in due season, in both respects. And therefore his care has been so effectual that he has not left this matter at loose ends. He has not contented himself with only saying, "Be kind one to another," knowing that a care that lies in everybody's hands equally is like to be neglected, but he has appointed officers, that his children may be fed in both body and soul as their necessities require.

The governors of all societies are wont to appoint officers for every public business that they look upon as of considerable importance, because experience teaches that otherwise it is not like to be effectually done. But such is the love of the Father of this spiritual family that he looks upon both their spiritual and outward supply as matters of great importance and therefore has appointed officers to take care of both. He has accounted their having outward supplies according to their necessities of such importance that he reckons their needs as his own, and their supplies as his own. He has taught us that he reckons what is done to one of the least of his brethren, he shall look upon as done to himself. The influence of his fatherly love and tenderness towards his church should be taken notice of by us and thankfully acknowledged and praised.

NOTES

1   Edwards deleted with a diagonal line: "And thus indeed it is in the officers of all societies. They are appointed to serve the society. Their business is in some respect to do good to the body of which they are officers."

2   See "Romans 12:7" in Matthew Henry, *An Exposition of All the Books of the Old and New Testament*, 6 vols. (London, 1708-1710).

6

EDITORS' INTRODUCTION

MINISTERS TO PREACH
NOT THEIR OWN WISDOM
BUT THE WORD OF GOD

When Edward Billing accepted a call from the church in Cold Spring (now Belchertown), Massachusetts, in February 1740, he asked his friend Jonathan Edwards to preach his ordination sermon. Billing graduated from Harvard College in 1731 and earned his M.A. in 1734. He spent the next few years filling pulpits in such Massachusetts towns as Hadley, where he preached in 1739.[1]

Edwards used the opportunity to mount a counterassault on what he saw as two of the greatest threats that the Enlightenment posed for Christianity. One threat was Arminianism, which claimed natural human ability to attain virtue through the freedom of the will and to discern the Bible's moral truth through reasonable interpretation. The other threat was Deism, a belief system that identified God's providence with natural law and elevated reason to the ultimate standard of belief.[2] Both Arminians and Deists held that the traditional interpretation of many scriptural texts contradicted reason. In such cases they relied on reason rather than Scripture. Edwards held that reason was reliable in its proper sphere. But God's revelation is a better guide to us than our own reason, Edwards insisted. Ministers, therefore, "are not to preach those things which their own wisdom or reason suggests, but the things already dictated to them by the superior wisdom and knowledge of God." Edwards exhorted Billing to preach God's Word rather than the dictates of his own reason, even when opponents should vilify him for it. He exhorted the congregation at Cold Spring to embrace submissively the doctrines of the Bible, even if they were mysterious and difficult to square with their own reason.

The manuscript, held by the Beinecke Rare Book and Manuscript Library, Yale University, consists of nineteen duodecimo leaves. On the first line of the first page, Edwards wrote, "Ordination of Mr. Billing. Appointed May 7, 1740." He also placed the symbol for his "History of Redemption" project in the first page's upper left-hand corner. Moreover, this sermon contains a selection that Edwards likely drew from "Miscellanies," No. 652, "Christian Religion. Mysteries in Religion."[3]

MINISTERS TO PREACH
NOT THEIR OWN WISDOM
BUT THE WORD OF GOD

1 CORINTHIANS 2:11-13

For what man knoweth the things of a man, save the spirit of man which is in him? even so the things of God knoweth no man, but the Spirit of God. Now we have received, not the spirit of the world, but the spirit which is of God; that we might know the things that are freely given to us of God. Which things also we speak, not in the words which man's wisdom teacheth, but which the Holy Ghost teacheth; comparing spiritual things with spiritual.

Corinth, the city where the Christians dwelt to whom this epistle was written, was one of the principal cities of Greece, a country that had been the chief seat of philosophy and learning and had been the most famed for human wisdom and the improvements of reason for many ages of any country in the world. It was but a little distant from Athens, the chief resort of philosophers in that land.

And many such were conversant in the city of Corinth itself. The apostle, in this epistle which he writes to the Christians in this city, considers the place that they lived in and accommodates what he writes to their circumstance. When the mysterious wonderful doctrines which the apostles taught concerning a crucified Jesus came abroad in the world and began to obtain footing in Greece as well as other countries, it was much taken notice of by the philosophers in Athens and Corinth and met with such a reception and treatment from them as might be expected from men that were so much conceited of and so much depended on their own reason as they did.

The strange doctrine of a crucified God, to their reason and philosophy, appeared very foolish, inconsistent, and ridiculous. As the apostle explained in the[4] eighteenth verse of the foregoing chapter, "For the preaching of the cross is to them that perish foolishness; but unto us which are saved it is the power of God." Verse 22, "the Greeks seek after wisdom." The Greek philosophers seek after something that shall be agreeable to their own reason.

But the gospel revelation concerning a crucified God was not so but appeared to them absurd and contrary to reason, as it follows: "But we preach Christ crucified, to the Jews a stumblingblock, and to the Greeks foolishness" [verse 23]. But the apostle observes that these philosophers, with all their boasted wisdom or reason, could never discern the truth in the things of God, and that this is done alone by the Gospel that they account inconsistent and self-contrary, and that God had made foolish their wisdom and baffled that human reason that they so much relied upon. Verses 19-21, "For it is written, I will destroy the wisdom of the wise, and will bring to nothing the understanding of the prudent. Where is the wise? where is the scribe? where is the disputer of this world? hath not God made foolish the wisdom of the world? For after that in the wisdom of God the world by wisdom knew not God, it pleased God by the foolishness of preaching to save them that believe." And the Gospel, which they called nonsense and foolishness, was wiser than their most boasted wisdom. Verse 25, "Because the foolishness of God is wiser than men; and the weakness of God is stronger than men."

They objected against those doctrines of the Gospel [for] their mysteriousness and unintelligibleness, and therefore in the sixth, seventh, [and] eighth verses of that chapter wherein is the text, we find "the wisdom of this world" and "of the princes of this world" and "the wisdom of God in a mystery" or "the hidden wisdom" set in opposition the one to the other. "Howbeit we speak wisdom among them that are perfect: yet not the wisdom of this world, nor of the princes of this world, that come to nought: but we speak the wisdom of God in a mystery, even the hidden wisdom, which God ordained before the world unto our glory: which none of the princes of this world knew: for had they known it, they would not have crucified the Lord of glory." By "the princes of this world" the apostle evidently means their philosophers and others that were accounted the wise and great men of the world. In the ninth and tenth verses, the apostle shows that it is no wonder that the things of the Gospel seem unintelligible and absurd to the wise men of the world. The reason he gives for it is that they are above our natural faculties, and our knowledge of them depends purely on the revelation made by the Spirit of God: "But as it is written, Eye hath not seen, nor ear heard, neither have entered into the heart of man, the things which God hath prepared for them that love him. But God hath revealed them unto us by his Spirit: for the Spirit searcheth all things, yea, the deep things of God." And in the words of the text this matter is further amplified, in which may be observed three things:

1. The reason is more particularly given why divine things are above man's reason and depend on pure revelation. The apostle very clearly illustrates it by a comparison taken from that which our daily experience teaches. We find that the things of men cannot be known by other men any further than they reveal or declare them. What we find within our own hearts our own spirits know, but no other men know them. Their reason will not help them to find out what we are conscious of within ourselves, unless we tell them.

So says the apostle it is with the things of God that we are told in the Gospel. They are things that concern God himself, his secret counsels and sovereign will, and things in himself which he alone can be supposed to see and be conscious to immediately. And therefore our reason will not help us to see them any further than God's Spirit is pleased to reveal.

2. We observe by what means the apostles and other Christians came to know them when they were above the reach of man's rea-

son, namely, by the revelation of God's Spirit. "Now we have received, not that spirit of the world," that is, the spirit of human wisdom, but things "freely given of God," the things of the Gospel.[5]

3. What foundation the apostle and other ministers went upon in teaching those things: They depended purely on divine revelation and not on human wisdom or philosophy. "Which things also we speak, not in the words which man's wisdom teacheth, but which the Holy Ghost teacheth." Their way was not first to compare the things that were revealed to the dictates and principles of philosophy which they or others had embraced and seemed right to their reason, but to compare them with other dictates or revelations of the Spirit, which is what the apostle means when he [says, "comparing spiritual things with spiritual"]. And then the apostle goes on in the three next verses further to give the reason why the mysteries of the Gospel appeared foolish and inconsistent to the philosophers and other natural men. "But the natural man receiveth not the things of the Spirit of God: for they are foolishness unto him: neither can he know them, because they are spiritually discerned. But he that is spiritual judgeth all things, yet he himself is judged of no man. For who hath known the mind of the Lord, that he may instruct him? But we have the mind of Christ" [verses 14-16].

DOCTRINE

Ministers are not to preach those things which their own wisdom or reason suggests, but the things already dictated to them by the superior wisdom and knowledge of God.

In handling this doctrine I would:

I. Show how the words of the doctrine are to be taken.

II. I would speak particularly to several things implied in the doctrine as belonging to the duty incumbent on a gospel minister.

I. I would briefly show how the words of the doctrine are to be taken, or what is meant when it is said that ministers are not to preach those things that their own wisdom suggests, but those things that are already dictated to them by the superior wisdom of God. Because it must be acknowledged that the words, as they may be taken, [are not true]: It is not true that ministers are not to preach those things that their own reason teaches, in the same manner as the apostle's doctrine, as it may be taken and perverted, is not true, namely, that ministers are not to preach what man's wisdom teaches [that is, there are some senses in which reason might legitimately suggest what ministers preach].

Therefore for the avoiding of all confusion that might arise from the misunderstanding of the words, I would particularly take notice of the various senses in which reason may be said to teach or suggest anything and show in what sense the words are to be taken when it is asserted that ministers are not to preach those things their own reason suggests.

There are three different senses in which reason may be said to teach or suggest things to man:

First. Reason may be said to dictate or teach these and those things, meaning by "reason" not the understanding or judgment of any man or men, but the reason and nature of things abstractly considered. There are many things that particular men's understandings or judgments dictate that reason, in this sense, does not dictate: For thus by reason is meant that in the nature of things that is or should be the object of the faculty, or rather the ground on which man's understanding should proceed in judging of things, rather than for any exercises of the faculty or the judgment itself that men make of things. It is something wholly independent of any judgments men make or anything that appears reasonable to one man or another. Reason in this sense is always infallible, for reason itself never teaches anything that is false. To suppose so would be to suppose that reason sometimes teaches that which [is] unreasonable or that which there is no good or just reason for, which is a contradiction.

Indeed, reason in this sense is nothing but another word for truth, or the evidence of truth, or good and just ground of our assent. And therefore it is not the meaning of the doctrine that ministers ought not to preach those things that reason suggests in this sense. It is not the design of the apostle, when he sets aside what man's wisdom teaches that he may establish what the Holy Ghost teaches, to set aside anything that true wisdom teaches or that which is wise in its own nature.

Second. Man's own reason may be said either directly or indirectly to dictate everything that he knows or believes by any means whatsoever. That is to say, man can know nothing but by the exercise of the faculty of reason. The mind of man cannot receive anything for truth but what it sees or thinks it sees, some reason to suppose to be truth.

That which men believe purely from the credit they give to others because others teach it and from the reliance they have on their superior understandings, yet they receive it as a thing which reason remotely and indirectly dictates to them. Their reason does not dictate it immediately and of it[self], but their reason suggests this, that those that testify it have sufficient knowledge of what they testify, and that they give a true testimony according to their knowledge. Their testimony is the argument that their reason relies upon, and so their reason does indirectly suggest it, though their reason of itself and independently suggests nothing of it.

So it is with respect to those things that men receive both by divine and human testimony. When men receive things as truth purely because God has revealed them, yet reason is remotely concerned, as it is by the faculty of reason that men know it to be a revelation, and by that faculty they know that a divine revelation is to be depended on.

Or if instead of the word *reason* we use the apostle's phrase and say "man's wisdom," there is nothing that men are to believe or teach but what is taught either directly or indirectly [by] their own best wisdom.

And therefore when the apostle would not have ministers preach those things that man's wisdom taught, this was not his meaning. He did not intend that ministers should not preach what man's best reason and wisdom indirectly taught them to be true because God had said it, for then he would not [have] made the distinction between the things that man's wisdom teaches and that the Holy Spirit teaches. But,

Third. Those things are more properly said to [be] dictates of man's own reason which their understanding or judgment suggests as acting of itself and not as being guided or led by the understanding of a teacher. These, for distinction's sake, may be called the dictates of man's reason. A man's reason, from the reliance reason has on the testimony and teaching of a superior understanding, may remotely suggest that which, at the same time, would be contrary to what their reason or judgment would suggest if it were left alone without such testimony. And it is so, in fact, in innumerable cases of human testimony as well as divine.

And this is doubtless the meaning of the apostle in the text and context when he sets what man's wisdom teaches and what the Holy Ghost teaches in contradistinction. And this is meant in the doctrine when it is said that ministers ought not to preach those things which their own wisdom or reason suggests, but the things that are already dictated by the Spirit of God. That is, they are not to preach those things that would seem right to their understandings if their understandings were left alone and acted independently of any testimony or teaching from the understanding of any other being. But in their preaching they ought to rely on what [is] revealed and discovered ready to their hands by an understanding infinitely superior to theirs. And this revelation they are to make the rule in their preaching.

Having thus explained the terms used in the doctrine, I proceed, in the

II. [Second place,] to speak particularly to several things implied in the doctrine as belonging to the duty incumbent on gospel ministers.[6]

First. It is their duty not to reject any doctrine that, by comparing one Scripture with another, appears truly to be held forth by the voice of revelation, though it contains difficulties and seeming inconsistencies that their reason cannot solve. We ought to receive doctrines that thus appear to be taught in Scripture, though they are mysteries—yea, though they remain mysteries to us still, that is, though they still contain what we cannot comprehend and still have difficulties remaining in them that we cannot solve. We are not to wait till they cease to be mysteries to us before we receive them for truth.

The apostle in the text and context does expressly oppose the way of the philosophers in Athens and Corinth who sought after wisdom, and of the Jews [who] required a sign and would believe nothing that their own wisdom or reason could not comprehend.

The apostle seems to blame those Greek philosophers that they did not receive the doctrine of Christ crucified, though to their reason it seemed foolishness—that is, though it contained seeming inconsistencies that their reason could not solve. 1 Corinthians 1:22-23, "For the Jews require a sign, and the Greeks seek after wisdom. But we preach Christ crucified, to the Jews a stumblingblock, and to the Greeks foolishness." That which men see no difficulty in but what their reason can solve, no seeming inconsistency at all, does not appear foolishness to them. And if they in those days ought to have received the doctrines of divine revelation, though they had seeming inconsistencies, then we ought to do so now. The apostle says, in the next verse after the text, that "the natural man receiveth not the things of the Spirit of God" (that is, the things of pure revelation), "for they are foolishness to him." But must we think therefore that the apostle supposed the natural man acted as reasonably in rejecting these doctrines as the spiritual man who received them?

It is unreasonable to expect any other in a divine revelation than that it should contain mysteries and things that, to our understanding, should be very difficult and seemingly inconsistent. If God will give us a revelation from heaven of the very truth concerning his own nature and acts, counsels, and ways and of the spiritual and invisible world, it is unreasonable to expect any other than that there should be many things in such a revelation that should be utterly beyond our understanding and seem impossible. For when was there ever a time when, if there had been a revelation from heaven of the very truth in philosophical matters and concerning the nature of created things, which must be supposed to lie more level with our understanding than divine things, but that there would have been many things in such a revelation that would have appeared not only to the vulgar but also to the learned men of that age absurd and impossible? If many of those positions in philosophy which are now received by the learned world as undoubted truths had been revealed from heaven to be truths in past ages, they would have been looked upon as mysterious and difficult and would seem as impossible as the most mysterious Christian doctrines do now.

And it is not reasonably to be questioned but that even now, after all the progress that is made in philosophy, if there should come a revelation from heaven of what is the very truth in these matters, without deviating at all from strict truth to accommodate its doctrine to our received notions and principles, there would be many things in it that, to our reason, would seem to be absurd and self-inconsistent. And I make no doubt but that there are learned men here present that do now receive principles in philosophy as certain and out of doubt which the day has been when if they had been then told them, they would have looked upon them [as] difficult as any mystery that is commonly supposed to be in the Bible.

Without doubt, much of the difficulty that we have about many of the doctrines of revelation are from wrong principles. We find that those things that are received as principles in one age and are never once questioned, it comes into nobody's thought that they possibly may not be true—and yet they are exploded in another age as light increases.

If God makes a revelation to us, he must reveal to us the truth as it is without accommodating himself to man's notions and principles, which would indeed be impossible, for those things which are received notions in one age are contrary to what are so in another. The wisdom of God was not given for any particular age, but for all ages. It surely therefore becomes us to receive what God reveals to be truth and to look upon his word as proof sufficient, whether what he reveals squares with our notions or not.

These things considered, and considering of how sublime nature divine things are which are the subjects about which divine revelation is conversant, it is not to be wondered at that that revelation contains mysteries. It is rather to be wondered at that it contains no more. It is probably because God is tender of us and has considered the weakness of our sight and reveals only such things as he sees a humble honest mind can well enough bear. Such a kind of tenderness we see in Christ towards his disciples, who had many things to say but forbore because they could not bear them.

Certainly those with whom difficulties and seeming inconsistencies are a weighty objection against any doctrines of revelation do not make suitable allowance for the vast disproportion there is between God's understanding and ours. There are some things—for instance, certain mathematical theorems that relate to quantity and measure—that are known to be true not only by men of learning but by other adult persons of good understanding, which yet if told to children appear very absurd and seem to imply great and evident contradictions. And certainly the wisest of us are but children to God. There is vastly a greater disproportion between the understanding of [God and] the oldest philosopher or mathematician than between his and that of the meanest child.[7]

It is unreasonable to think any other than that many things appear to ourselves exceeding difficult and incomprehensible while our faculties are in the present low state, [but] that may all be unfolded and seem easy in some future state of a higher elevation of our faculties. If one looks for anything in the dark by so low a faculty as the sense of feeling or by seeing with a dim light, sometimes we cannot find it and it will seem impossible that it should be there; but yet when a clear light comes to shine into the place and we discern by a better faculty, or by the same faculty under better advantage, the thing that before was investigable[8] appears very plain to us.

Nor do those who insist on such objections against any doctrine taught by divine revelation duly consider what must necessarily be supposed to arise from the sublime nature of divine things, about which divine revelation is conversant. Christ says to Nicodemus, John 3:12, "If I have told you earthly things, and ye believe not, how shall ye believe, if I tell you of heavenly things?" Plainly intimating that it is reasonable to suppose truths concerning heavenly things or things that in their own nature are much more above us should contain much greater difficulties and mysteries than those things that are earthly and are of a lower nature, that are more proportioned to our understanding. There are two things that are plain from these remarkable words of Christ:

1. That that tenet which some of late have advanced, that there are no mysteries in religion, is false. Christ's words imply that there are things contained in those doctrines that he came into the world to teach that are mysterious, not only in that sense that they are above a perfect comprehension, but also in that sense that they are difficult to the judgment or belief, as containing seeming impossibilities difficult to be believed, on the same account that the doctrine of the new birth was difficult to Nicodemus, as he expressed himself in the ninth verse, to which those words of Christ are a reply: "How can these things be?" implying that they seemed to him impossible. And,

2. The words also plainly imply that the more persons or beings are in their own nature above us, the more are doctrines or truths concerning them mysterious to us and difficult to our reason, [and] the more do those things that are really true concerning them contain seeming inconsistencies and impossibilities, implying that if Nicodemus said "How can these things be?" or "How is it possible?" when Christ had told him earthly things, much more would he say so if he should tell him heavenly things.

When men will reject doctrines merely because their reason cannot reconcile the difficulties that are in them, though otherwise they seem plainly to be doctrines contained in the Scriptures, certainly [it] must be from secret pride and atheism of heart; for men do in fact commonly give one another greater credit than such men do God omniscient. As we see when any person that we have long known and had much experience of his discretion and veracity testify to us any matter of fact as what they have been eyewitnesses to and have had full and certain knowledge of, and especially if there be many that testify, though it seems a very strange thing to us and we do not see how it is possible that it should be, yet how ready are we to suspect our understanding in such cases and to submit to the force and weight of their positive testimony, though still the matter [is] a great mystery with us.

And even in things that are not matters of fact but matters of judgment, how ready are men to trust to the determinations of a man universally reputed a man of a great genius, of vast penetration and insight into things, if he is positive in anything that appears mysterious to us and is quite contrary to what we thought ourselves clear and certain in before. How are we ready in such a case to suspect ourselves, especially if it be a matter wherein he has been very much versed and has had much more occasion to look into it than we, and under greater advantages to know the truth. And why then do not we yield a submission that is in some sort proportionable to that Being in comparison of whom the greatest earthly genius is an infant and a worm, and his understanding foolishness and darkness?

Second. Ministers are not to make those things that seem right to their own reason a rule in their interpreting a revelation, but the revelation is to be the rule of its own interpretation. That is, the way that they must interpret Scripture is not to compare the dictates of the Spirit of God in his revelation with what their own reason says and then to force such an interpretation as shall be agreeable to those dictates, but they must interpret the dictates of the Spirit of God by comparing them with other dictates of that Spirit. As the apostle is express[ing] in the text, they must teach the things the Holy Ghost teaches, "comparing spiritual things with spiritual." We must interpret the Scripture by itself, and not by the dictates of our own hearts.

Thus to make what seems right to our reason our rule in interpreting the Scriptures is still to make our mere reason our highest rule in our search after truth, and God's revelation but a subordinate rule; which certainly is to suppose that our own mere reason is a better rule or a better guide to us than God's revelation, which is contrary to what all that pretend to revealed religion suppose to be the ground of the necessity of a revelation, which is the great imperfection and darkness of man's reason in his fallen state, which makes us to stand in need of a better guide. But if, when the revelation is given, it is [to] be no better a guide, but still reason is the best guide and the superior rule, then how is this defect supplied by a better guide? Revelation was given to be [a] rule to reason, a guide to our understanding, and not our understanding to be a guide and rule to that. If man's own reason be a superior rule to revelation, we stand in no need of a revelation, having a rule that is better already, and it is not worth the while to expect one or admit one.

Indeed, reason must be used in judging whether a pretended revelation be indeed a divine revelation. But when reason has once received and established this, that it is indeed a revelation from God's infinite, infallible understanding, it is unreasonable after[wards] not to make it a rule to our infinitely inferior reason and to receive it with all its mysteries and difficulties without wresting it at all to conform it to our reason. If a pretended revelation has not credit or evidence enough to be received with all the difficulties that are reasonably to be expected in a divine revelation, and such as, comparing one part of it with another, we find to be indeed contained in it, it has not evidence enough to be received as a divine revelation at all.

This method of first determining what is agreeable to reason and then interpreting the Scripture by it is making the Scripture wholly of no use to us in those things wherein we so interpret it. The Scripture manifests nothing; it declares nothing at all; the manifestation is from something else, namely, reason, and the Scripture is only a clog to that manifestation. Without it, we should have but one thing to do, namely, to determine what the voice of reason was. But now we have double work: first, to determine what the voice of reason is, and then to find out a way how to interpret the Scripture agreeable to it. The Deists, that wholly reject revelation and will have no rule but reason, act more reasonably than those who receive revelation [only] to set another rule over it. If we will not rely upon a revelation when we have embraced it, let us disclaim it as not worthy of being regarded as such.[9]

Third. Ministers are not only not to reject those doctrines of revelation that are difficult to their reason themselves, but are to teach them to their hearers. To say as some do concerning these and those mysterious doctrines that are taught in the Holy Scriptures, that they are things that are attended with great difficulties and are hard to be understood, that have puzzled the heads of the most learned divines, and therefore it is imprudent for ministers to meddle with them in their preaching; there are plain practical truths enough for them to insist on; it is not best for ministers to trouble their people's heads with matters of such nice speculation: To say this is greatly to reproach the wisdom of God and to make ourselves wiser than he. God in his wisdom thought it best that those mysterious doctrines should be taught, otherwise to what purpose did he teach them? Or else we must return to the tenet of the Papists, who suppose the Scriptures were given only for the learned men, and that there are so many things that are mysterious in [them] that it is not fit to be in the hands of the common people, and therefore do not suffer them to have the Scriptures in a known tongue. And certainly if those doctrines be not fit to be taught the common people, the divines of our nation have done very imprudently in translating those parts of the Scripture that contain them into English.

If God had left it to ministers' discretion what doctrines they had best to teach their people, it would be another case. But God has not done so. Ministers are only sent on his errand. God has not left it to their discretion what their errand shall be. They are to preach the preaching that he bids them (Jonah 3:2). He has put into their hands a Book containing a summary of doctrine and bids them go and preach that Word. And what daring presumption would it be for them afterwards to pick and choose among the doctrines contained in that summary and to say, "These are fit for me to preach, and these are not fit; this part of my errand is fit to be done, and this not"?

God does not need to be told by his messengers what message is fit to deliver to those to whom he sends them, but they are to declare his counsel and are not to shun to declare his whole counsels, whether men will hear or whether they will forbear. Acts 20:27, "For I have not shunned to declare to you all the counsel of God."

APPLICATION

[The application] may be in one or two inferences, and a brief exhortation.

First [Inference]. Hence we learn [that] that rule of interpreting Scripture so much insisted upon by many of late, namely, first to determine by our own reason what is agreeable to the moral perfections of God and then to interpret the Scriptures by them, is an unjust and fallacious one. Thus to do is certainly to do the thing that has already been shown to be absurd, namely, to make the dictates of our own reason the highest rule in judging of the things of God and to make it a rule to revelation itself. Reason is to determine that there is a God, and that he is an infinitely perfect holy Being, and that the Scripture is his Word. But when we have determined this, modesty and humility and reverence to God require that we allow that God is better able to declare to us what is agreeable to that perfection than we are to declare to him or ourselves. Reason tells us that God is just, but God is better able to tell what acts are agreeable to that justice than we are.

The supreme legislative authority of a nation does not ask children what laws are just for them to make or what rules are just for them to proceed by, nor do they wait for the judgment and determination of every subject in order to oblige them to submission. Much less does the infinitely great and wise sovereign of heaven and earth wait for the decision of our judgment and reason [as to] what laws or rules of proceeding in him are just, in order to require our submission to him.

Divine revelation in these things does not go abegging for credit and validity by approbation and applause of our understanding. On the contrary, the style in which these revelations are often given forth is this: "Thus saith the Lord," and "I am the Lord," and "He that hath an ear to hear, let him hear," and "Who art thou, O man, that repliest against God?"

If that be a good rule now to reject whatsoever to our reason does not seem agreeable to the moral perfections of God, then it always was so. And then why does the apostle mention such an objection that some in his days made against something in divine revelation as unreasonable, as in Romans 9:19, "Why does he yet find fault? For who hath resisteth his will?" That is mentioned as an objection of some against something in divine revelation—whatever that was—and the objection was that they could not see how it was agreeable to the moral perfections in God. But yet the apostle sharply reproves it as a daring presumptuous objection. "Nay," says he, "but, O man, who art thou that repliest against God? Shall the thing formed say to him that formed it, Why hast thou made me thus?" [Romans 9:20].

Second [*Inference*]. If ministers ought to proceed by such a rule in their preaching, no wonder that such confusion has followed on their proceeding by a contrary rule. Seeing that man's own reason, blind as it is, has of late been so much set up as man's highest rule in judging of divine things—and even a rule superior to revelation itself—no wonder that Arminianism and Arianism, Deism and atheism have come in like a deluge. When once men come to that, as to set up their reason as their highest rule, it is no wonder that they hasten to the same state of darkness that they were in when they had no other rule, when they had no revelation and nothing else to guide them but their own reason, when they were in a state of heathenism.

When men come to make God's revelation to be only the handmaid or bondmaid, and to set reason over it as its mistress, no wonder that it soon comes to that, that the mistress casts out the bondmaid and all her progeny, insisting that the mistress's offspring shall inherit alone.

[*Exhortation.*] Before I conclude, I would address myself in a few words to those that are more immediately concerned in the solemn affair of this day. And,

1. To the person that is to be set apart to the sacred work of the gospel ministry this day: Sir, I would now humbly and earnestly recommend to you that Holy Book which God is about to commit into your hands, as containing that message which you are to deliver to this people in his name. God gives you this Word—which is his

Word—to preach that, and not the dictates of your own reason. You are to preach the dictates of God's infinitely superior understanding, humbly submitting your reason as a learner and disciple to that, renouncing all confidence in your own wisdom and entirely relying on God's instructions.

God is now about to deliver to you a summary of doctrines already discovered and dictated to your hand, which you are to teach and zealously to maintain. And if the time should come that you should be reproached for so doing, with such kind of reproaches as are in these days commonly cast on such as earnestly preach the mysterious doctrines of revelation, and you should be called a bigoted zealot, one whose zeal runs before your knowledge, one that durst not indulge a freedom of thought, one that dare not presume to think otherwise than your forefathers thought, one of those that judge of God by themselves, that think that God is a morose, ill-natured sort of being because they are so, one that is a person of little sense or reason—if such proud contemptuous reproaches are cast upon you, merely because you rely more on God's testimony than the dictates of your own reason, the time will soon come when they will be wiped away. Your Lord and Master, that commanded you to preach those doctrines, will defend you and will show in his time who has proceeded with greatest wisdom: you [who] have relied on God's wisdom, or they who have been wise in their own eyes and have leaned to their own understanding and have despised others, that have not trusted more to God's instructions.

2. Let me now earnestly beseech God's people in this place— many of which I have special cause to be concerned for by reason of the distinct relations I have heretofore stood in towards them[10]— when they have such doctrines delivered to them from the Word of God as are mysterious and difficult to their reason, nevertheless meekly to receive them as the Word of God. Do not allow yourselves in a caviling, objecting disposition. Consider how that God is infinitely wiser than men. You are certainly safe in following his instructions, however mysterious his instructions are, and there is no safety in any other way. For you to oppose your reason to God's Word is

the way for you to go backwards and fall and be broken and snared and taken, to fall into utter confusion and ruin.

And if you should be ridiculed by others in this day of growing error for embracing certain doctrines of revelation that are above man's comprehension, as if you were fools and put out your eyes to receive absurd doctrines by an implicit faith, care not for it, but be willing to become fools for Christ's sake, remembering that he that would be wise must become a fool, that he may be wise and glory in that which they call your foolishness, which you have by God's instruction, remembering that "the foolishness of God is wiser than men."

In thus adhering to the Word of God rather than your own wisdom, both pastor and people shall hereafter shine forth as the sun in the kingdom of your Father and shall appear to be some of those truly wise that shall shine as the brightness of the firmament.

NOTES

1 Sylvester Judd, *The History of Hadley, Massachusetts* (1905; reprint, Somersworth, NH: New Hampshire Publishing Company, 1976), 320. For more on Billing, see John Langdon Sibley, *Biographical Sketches of Graduates of Harvard University, in Cambridge, Massachusetts* (Cambridge, MA: Charles William Sever, 1873), 22-28.

2 For a more extensive discussion of the setting and content of this sermon, see Kenneth P. Minkema and Richard A. Bailey, eds., "Reason, Revelation, and Preaching: An Unpublished Ordination Sermon by Jonathan Edwards," in *Southern Baptist Journal of Theology* 3:2 (Summer 1999): 16-33.

3 See this entry in Jonathan Edwards, *The "Miscellanies" 501-832*, ed. Ava Chamberlain, Vol. 18 of *Works of Jonathan Edwards* (New Haven, CT: Yale University Press, 2000), 192-193.

4 Edwards deleted the following with diagonal lines: "so that they treated it with the like haughty contempt as many that call themselves men of reason in these days do those doctrines of divine revelation which are above their reason and beside their philosophy. Therefore the drift of the Apostle throughout this chapter and the latter part of the foregoing, is to show the vanity of man's wisdom or reason when he set up in opposition to or competition with this divine revelation which God has given in the Gospel. He observes how the Greek philosophers objected against the doctrine of a crucified Lord and Savior as foolish and inconsistent."

5 Edwards deleted the following with a series of diagonal lines: "By 'spirit of the world' the Apostle means the spirit of human wisdom and philosophy, as is evident by the context."

6 Edwards made two false starts on this head, which he deleted with vertical lines:

"1. It is their duty not to reject any doctrine that, by comparing one Scripture with another, appears really to be held forth by the voice of revelation, though their own reason does not teach it."

"1. It is their duty not to reject any doctrine that is taught by divine revelation, though man's reason does not teach it. If men are to receive no doctrines of revelation that are above reason, or none that are taught by revelation but what their reason can reach and teaches them in the first place, [this] is to render a revelation wholly useless, and indeed makes it in effect to be no revelation: for nothing is revealed, nor is anything at all received, because it is revealed by God, but because it is taught by man's own reason; and then there is no need of its being revealed in order to its being revealed. If no doctrine is to be received but what reason teaches, then men must first see whether their reason teaches it before they receive it. And at this rate, it is impossible that God's revelation should ever really be the ground of our receiving any one doctrine whatsoever, because no doctrine is received till we have first consulted reason to know whether that teaches it: so that our receiving it is always in this way prior to our hearing the voice of revelation; so that the foundation of our faith is man's reason or wisdom, and not divine revelation, in direct opposition to the rule of the Apostle in the fifth verse of the context: 'that your faith should not stand in the wisdom of men, but in the power of God.'"

7 This passage could well have been drawn from "Miscellanies," No. 652, "Christian Religion. Mysteries in Religion" (c. 1734), in which Edwards was responding to the objection that revelation contains many things beyond the scope of human reason. In the entry, Edwards described how he demonstrated to a thirteen-year-old boy the apparently mysterious fact "that a piece of matter two inches square was eight times so big as one but one inch square." The final sentence of the entry bears a striking similarity to the final sentence of this paragraph: "Doubtless, there is a vastly greater distance between our understanding and God's, than between this boy's and that of the greatest philosopher or mathematician."

8 Archaic for "undiscoverable" or "unsearchable."

9 Edwards deleted the following with a vertical line: "Though we make the dictates of man's reason to have the force of a rule in interpreting Scripture, and so to make it comply with reason, wrest it from the proper signification of the words as appearing by comparing Scripture with Scripture, treat God so as it would be accounted ridiculous to treat men. Whenas men whose language and manner of speaking we have been acquainted with."

10 Cold Spring, later Belchertown, was originally settled in 1737 in part by inhabitants of Northampton.

7

EDITORS' INTRODUCTION

PASTOR AND PEOPLE
MUST LOOK TO GOD

On January 21, 1741, Edwards delivered this sermon—"to the great satisfaction of the people"—at a fast preceding the ordination of Chester Williams as pastor of the church at Hadley, Massachusetts.[1] The church's previous pastor, seventy-year-old Isaac Chauncey, had ministered there since 1696, but in recent years had grown too weak to preach regularly. For several years the church invited various preachers, including Edward Billing, to supply their pulpit.[2] In November 1740, the church invited Chester Williams to settle among them as their pastor. Williams doubted their ability to maintain the level of support promised, which included ten acres of land, three hundred pounds in money, an annual salary of one hundred and forty pounds (to be increased to one hundred and eighty pounds after Chauncey died), and a sufficiency of firewood, but he accepted. His reply suggests the tension that ministers and people felt between the minister's spiritual aims and his material needs.

> Yet being unwilling to insist on any terms that should look unreasonable or mercenary or that threaten the peace of this place, but desiring only to be supported as it shall be for a min-

ister's honor and the honor of the people, hoping I covet you more than yours, I accept of your call upon the terms you have proposed, having confidence in your honor, justice, and readiness to do for my support at all times as my circumstances shall call for, and shall appear to be your duty. Begging your united prayers, that I may come to you always in the fullness of the blessing of the Gospel of Christ, and be a faithful and successful laborer in this part of his harvest.[3]

Williams remained Hadley's pastor until his death in 1753. In 1750 he sat on the council that advised the Northampton church to dismiss Edwards—he voted against Edwards.

In this sermon Edwards insisted that "the solemn setting apart of one to the work and office of a gospel minister" demands that pastor and people should pray earnestly for God's blessing. The "business of the Gospel is properly a divine business," Edwards said, and its success therefore depends in a direct manner on God's blessing. He also called the people to think much of their salvation, implored both minister and people to live peacefully together, charged the people to encourage their minister materially and spiritually, and exhorted the congregation to submit to their new minister.

———

This manuscript, held by the Beinecke Rare Book and Manuscript Library, Yale University, consists of fourteen duodecimo leaves. On the top line of the first page, Edwards wrote, "Fast at Hadley preceding ordination Jan[uary] 1740/41."

PASTOR AND PEOPLE
MUST LOOK TO GOD

ACTS 14:23

And when they had ordained them elders in every church, and had prayed with fasting, they commended them to the Lord, on whom they believed.

The apostles Paul and Barnabas had lately preached the Gospel in those three cities, Lystra, Iconium, and Antioch, and had had great success there and had converted many from heathenism to Christianity. And being now about to depart from them and to return to Antioch in Syria from whence they had been sent forth, we have an account in the text and foregoing verses of the care they took that religion might be upheld and might flourish, and their souls' welfare provided for after they were gone, which consisted in three things: in exhorting them, [in] praying with and for them, and in appointing proper officers in the churches. We have an account of the first of these, namely, their counseling and exhorting them, in the preceding verse: "confirming the souls of the disciples, and exhorting them to continue in their faith, and that we must through much tribulation enter into the kingdom of God." In the text we have an account of the two latter, where is observable,

1. The provision that the apostles made of proper means for the future flourishing of religion in these cities. They ordained them elders in every church.

2. Their earnest seeking to God for the success of those means. They prayed and fasted and so commended them to the Lord, on whom they believed. There is reason to think that the fasting and praying here spoken of was what attended the ordination of those elders, partly from the manner of expression: "And when they had ordained them elders in every church, and had prayed with fasting, they commended them to the Lord, on whom they believed." It is most natural to suppose that this ordination and prayer and fasting were conjoined in fact, as they are here in the relation, and partly from what appears to have been the manner of Christians in those times. Imposition of hands solemnly to separate persons to the work of the ministry was wont then to be joined with prayer and fasting, as appears in another instance that we have an account of in the beginning of the thirteenth chapter of this book: "Now there were in the church that was at Antioch certain prophets and teachers; as Barnabas, and Simeon that was called Niger, and Lucius of Cyrene, and Manaen, which had been brought up with Herod the tetrarch, and Saul. As they ministered to the Lord, and fasted, the Holy Ghost said, Separate me Barnabas and Saul for the work whereunto I have called them. And when they had fasted and prayed, and laid their hands on them, they sent them away." As Barnabas and Saul themselves had a little before received imposition of hands, attended with prayer and fasting, so now they lay hands on others as separating them to the work of the ministry. They also do [this] with prayer and fasting in like manner.

OBSERVATION

The solemn setting apart of one to the work and office of a gospel minister is an affair wherein God should earnestly be sought to.

Prayer is a duty wherein we seek to God for his favors and blessing upon us. And when fasting is joined with prayer, it is that God may be sought to in that duty with the greater earnestness, that we may the more entirely separate ourselves from all worldly concerns and worldly delights, that so our whole souls may be engaged in seeking to God, with confession of our unworthiness of the mercies that we humbly and importunately [are] calling upon him for.

I would speak to this observation in the following method:

I. I would show by whom God should be earnestly sought to on such an occasion;

II. What they are earnestly [to] seek to God for; and,

III. Why God should earnestly [be] sought to on such an occasion.

I. It may be inquired who they are that should earnestly seek to God on such an occasion.

First. He is earnestly to be sought to by him that is to be set apart to this sacred office, who is above all others concerned in this affair, being the person that is to be the immediate subject of this solemn transaction, and therefore is the person whom it chiefly concerns to have the presence, smiles, and blessing of God in it.

Second. God is on such an occasion earnestly to be sought to by the people that call him to that work and among whom he is solemnly ordained to and settled in that work. They also are very nearly concerned in this affair. It is on their desire and invitation that he is solemnly set apart to that work, and it is principally for their sakes. The work that he is set apart to is to lead and feed their souls. Their everlasting good is the direct design of the affair.

Third. God should earnestly be sought to by neighboring churches, and especially neighboring pastors, whose proper work and business it is solemnly to set them apart to their office. Though it by far the most nearly concerns the people over whom they are ordained, yet the settlement of a minister in any place does also much concern neighboring churches. For by reason of that intercourse and mutual concern that the circumstances of neighboring churches naturally and necessarily lead them to, and which also rules of Christian charity and communion oblige them to, neighboring churches are interested in each other's welfare. If one is corrupted, it tends to disturb and infect the rest. And if one flourishes and prospers, it naturally tends to the health of the rest. Neighboring churches do, by virtue of the tendency of human nature, and from the general circumstances of mankind, together with the general rules of the Gospel, as it were naturally in some sort become one body. And doubtless it is most agreeable to reason and Christianity that churches in various neighborhoods should unite themselves in bodies and societies, as the circumstance of their habitation and vicinity shall render most convenient, for mutual assistance in that great business and work common to all Christian churches—the service and worship of God, and to promote the common cause of Christ's kingdom and the flourishing of religion.

Especially does the affair of the settlement of a minister concern neighboring ministers, as they are to be fellow laborers and fellow helpers in the same great work. Hence in the Holy Scriptures we read of presbyteries, which it is most natural to understand of elders or presbyters in a neighborhood formed into societies to assist one another in the affairs of the ministerial function, and particularly the ordination of ministers, who, as they are therefore to be immediately concerned in the affair of the solemn setting apart [of] ministers in churches in their vicinity, so should be concerned earnestly to look to God and to seek his blessing in such an affair.

II. What God is to be earnestly sought to for by those that are concerned in this great affair. I answer in two things, namely, first, for his presence or assistance in the affair, and, second, his blessing upon it and the success of it.

First. God is earnestly to be sought to for his presence in the management of the affair. That is, God is to be sought to, to grant the influences of his Spirit, that the affair may be managed in such a manner as shall be to his acceptance and glory.

As it is a great and very solemn transaction, so it is much to be desired that it may be faithfully performed to the acceptance of that great and holy God in whose name it is performed, that it may be performed with suitable humility and sense of the divine majesty and our dependence on God, and from respect to the glory of God.

God is to be sought to for his presence with the person that is to be separated, that he may be enabled to undertake the work with a sense of the greatness, importance, and difficulty of the work, a sense of his own unworthiness and insufficiency, and a dependence on

Christ, the Great Shepherd of the sheep; and that he may be enabled to give up himself to this work with his whole heart, and to give up himself to God in it, as mainly seeking the advancement of the kingdom of his great Lord and Master that sends him, and the good of precious souls, and not for filthy lucre or an outward support or from regard to his temporal interests.

God is also to be sought to for his presence with the people, that they and the pastor ordained over them may give up themselves to the Lord and to each other by the will of God, that they may consider what the great ends of their settlement of a minister among them are, and may act with a sincere aim at and earnest desire of these ends and humble dependence on God for success.

And God is to be sought to for his presence with those elders that are concerned in the solemn separation of the person to this work, that as they act in the name of the great head of the church in it, so they may act in his fear and love and with a believing dependence upon him.

Second. God is earnestly to be sought to for the success of this affair, or that the great ends of it may be obtained, that the person set apart may be furnished for his great work and ever assisted in it, and that the people may always do their duty in supporting and encouraging and strengthening the hands of their pastor and diligently attending to and improving his ministry, and that the blessed Spirit of God may abundantly attend his ministration for the gloriously advancing [of] the kingdom of Christ in that place and the salvation of multitudes of souls. I come now,

III. To inquire for what reasons God should earnestly be sought to for those things on such an occasion. The main reasons may be summed up under these three heads, namely, the vast importance of this affair, the special relation it has to God, and the special dependence of the good management and success of it on the divine influence and blessing.

First. God should be earnestly sought to in this affair because of the vast importance of it. God is to be acknowledged and sought to in all our concerns, but especially in those of great moment. It is surely no more than decent and an honor that belongs to the great possessor and governor of the world that we should go to him and ask his favor in all important affairs, and the more solemnly and earnestly according as the affair is more important. And not only the honor of God, but our own interest requires it.

Now it is of vast importance that God's favor and blessing should be obtained in such an affair as the settling of a gospel minister. It is of great importance to the church of God in general that it should be furnished with able, faithful, and successful ministers. And it is especially of vast importance to that people that are settling a minister among them. It is difficult to think of any affair that a people are ever concerned in of equal importance. It most nearly concerns them as to their greatest interest, even their eternal interest, the everlasting salvation of themselves and their children. If a people are favored and blessed in it, they are like to be everlasting gainers by it. The salvation of many souls from going down to the pit of eternal destruction, and bringing them to everlasting glory, is like to be the issue, so that they will be happy here and forever. But if a people are not blessed in this affair, they are like to be a miserable people. The consequence is like to be the perishing of multitudes, their being miserable here and miserable forever.

If God favors a people in this affair, then he himself will dwell with them and be their God, and happy is the people that is in such a case. But if a people are not blessed in it, it is an awful token and fruit of God's anger. It is because he has not blessings in store for them.

A good minister that has the presence of God with him in his work is the very greatest blessing that ever God bestows upon a people, next to himself. We read that Christ ascended on high and received gifts for men, among which gospel ministers are mentioned as the chief (Ephesians 4:8-11). And Christ never gives a greater blessing to a people excepting when he gives himself. And indeed the giving himself is implied in giving a faithful and successful minister.

It tends to the happiness of a people in this world. It tends very much even to their outward comfort and welfare. It tends to the maintaining of peace and good order amongst a people. It tends to promote moral and Christian virtues, which above all other things in the world exalt a people and make them honorable and happy. It tends [to] a great deal of spiritual joy and comfort to a people. It tends to make God's sabbaths pleasant days, and to make his house a pleasant place to them, and to make them delight in his ordinances and rejoice in Christian communion one with another. And then it tends to their peace and comfort on a death-bed and their eternal peace and glory in another world.

It tends not only to the happiness of the present generation but of the children yet to be born. And religion and both temporal and spiritual prosperity will be likely to be transmitted as an inheritance from one generation to another.

But if a people be not blessed in this affair, it tends, as we see by experience in many instances, to make them a miserable people. It makes the offering of the Lord to be abhorred; it occasions everything to be in a state of confusion and is oftentimes the undoing of both the present and the future generations, both for time and eternity.

It is also of vast importance to the person that is to be set apart to this work that he should have the favor and blessing of God in it. And particularly that he should obtain grace to be faithful in it, that he may be a wise and faithful steward that may sincerely love his Master and seek his glory and the good of precious souls, and may comfort others with the comforts {of the Gospel}, that he may both save himself and them that hear him, that after he has preached to others, he himself may not be cast away. If it should be otherwise, if he should not be faithful in his work so as to [be] accepted of his great Master another day, he will eternally rue it that ever he undertook that work.

Unfaithful ministers, as one says, little think how they are drawing up their own indictments when they are composing their sermons. No order of men have such advantage to know their Lord's will and are under such obligations to do it as gospel ministers, and none will be so much condemned out of their own mouths. And probably the wicked of no one order of men whatsoever will have so low a place in hell [as] unfaithful and wicked ministers.

Therefore, this great work should be entered upon with fear and trembling, and God should be humbly and earnestly sought to by those that are about to enter upon it for his grace and favor in it, whereby they may be enabled to serve him in it with a gracious sincerity and fidelity.

Second. On the account of the special relation that this affair has to God. The business of the Gospel is properly a divine business. They that are called to this work are called to a work that may properly be called Christ's work. It is a business wherein a person has, in all parts of it, to do with God. It is either to act in the name of God's people towards God, or in the name of God towards the people. It all consists in acting either to God or from God. And it is to act for God. God is more immediately the end of the work of the ministry than of any other work or employment that men are called to in this world. When a people call a minister, it is that he may be a person by whom they may carry on their affairs to Godward—a person to act for them before God, and by whom they may worship him. The office of the ministry is an office not of any human or earthly kingdom, but it is an office of Christ's kingdom. A gospel minister is Christ's officer, and his business is to be an instrument to carry on Christ's work, the work of redemption.

Surely, therefore, it is most decent that God should be appealed to in this affair. Would it be decent to manage the affair of appointing or setting apart stewards and other officers in the house of a king without applying to the king in this affair? Is it decent to go about to appoint officers in the church of Christ without making application to the head of the church? Or to send forth laborers into the harvest without seeking to the Lord of the harvest?

Third. The third reason why God should be earnestly sought to in this affair is the special dependence of the success of it on the divine influence and blessing. Men depend on God's blessing and favorable providence for success in all affairs, but the dependence of the success of this affair on God's influence is more manifold and more immediate.

It depends on God every way. It is he that must furnish and qualify a minister for his work. It is he that must give a heart sincerely and earnestly to seek the ends of it. It is he that must assist him in private and in public. It is he that must dispose a minister well to his people, and it is he that must incline their hearts well to him, and so influence both, that good understanding may be kept up between minister and people that may make way for the success of his ministry.

And after all, it is he that by the immediate influence of his Spirit must actually give the success. All endeavors for prosperity in this affair without God's blessing will be in vain. Psalm 127:1, "Except the Lord do build the house, they labor in vain that build it: except the Lord do keep the city, the watchman waketh but in vain."

There is great opposition made against a people prospering in this great affair by the enemies of Christ and souls. The devil endeavors to his utmost to bring a blast on such affairs. And we see how often he is successful, either by leading ministers into corrupt opinions or into vice, or by alienating the hearts of a people from their minister and sowing discord between them.

The many fatal examples we see of this kind, one would think, should make a people that are about to settle a minister earnest in seeking to God, that he would be pleased to favor and smile upon and bless them in this great affair.

APPLICATION

I come now briefly [to] apply what has been said to the affair of the present day, which has been set apart by God's people in this place as a day of solemn fasting and prayer, to seek to God for his blessing upon them in the affair of the settlement of a minister.

And I would earnestly exhort you now, and at all times, to look to God and earnestly to seek to him and wait upon him for his presence with you and [his] smiles upon you in this great affair, that now there may be a foundation for much of the greatest good to you and your children. If God is pleased to bless you and succeed you in this affair, that alone will make you a happy people and will be far better to you than if he bestowed upon you thousands of gold and silver.

Therefore, now let those that have any interest at the throne of grace improve it and wrestle with God for so great a mercy. And not only now, but let it be your steadfast and earnest request and suit at the throne of grace. Yea, let all cry to God for it. Those that are saints will be disposed to it. Their love to Christ and desire of the flourishing of his kingdom, as well as regard to their own souls, will stir them up to it.

And those that are sinners, that are yet in a Christless condition, surely had need [that is, ought] earnestly [to] seek this of God. For if God does not bless this people in this affair and does not succeed the work of the ministry, there will be so much greater danger of their everlasting perdition.

You are now going about an affair that is of great concern to you, which, however regardless and unconcerned some may be about [it], yet without doubt it will in its issue prove an affair of vast consequence to everyone that shall live under the ministry of him that is about to be set apart to that sacred work among you. It will in all probability infinitely alter the case one way or the other with respect to everyone. Either it will be an affair that will issue in his eternal benefit or will be for the aggravation of his eternal misery, according as you in particular are blessed in this affair or otherwise. Therefore, let none be indifferent, but let God be earnestly sought to by all. And here for direction,

I. Do not mock God by a pretense of fasting and prayer and earnestly seeking to God for his blessing in this affair when at the same time you neglect the salvation of your own soul. How inconsistently with yourself will you act if you fast and pray on such an occasion as this and at the same time are so unconcerned about the salvation of your soul as to live in known sins and in the willful neglect of secret prayer and other duties and necessary means of your salvation. Your pretense in fasting and prayer on this occasion is that the minister you are about to settle may be an instrument of your soul's salvation, but what a mockery of God is this if at the same time you are indeed not so much concerned about your salvation, but that you live in the daily, willful neglect of those things that you know are required in order to your salvation. If you continue to live careless, unawakened, and slothful in the business of religion, you never will be saved, let you have what minister you will—though he should come to you with the tongue of men and angels. If you should live under the most eminent minister that ever lived, it will only aggravate your damnation.

In all that such persons do in the affair of the settlement of a minister, they are inconsistent with themselves. When they agree with a minister for such a settlement and salary, they are only bargaining for means of their condemnation. They do but pay so much money for the better place in hell and are at great expense for double damnation.

II. If you seek to God to bless you in the settlement of a minister, then carefully watch against whatever might arise between minister and people to hinder his being a blessing to you. And particularly, to your utmost watch against misunderstanding and prejudices between minister and people. A minister should carefully avoid giving any just occasion and lightly taking up prejudices against any of his flock.

And a people should stand at the greatest distance from anything that might tend to beget in them a prejudice against him, for this will exceedingly tend utterly to frustrate his ministry as to them. You had better leave the town, though it should be greatly to your temporal loss. You had better live poor and fare hardly out of town than live highly and in great fullness in it with a rooted prejudice against your minister.

Let other calamities be a warning to you. How has contention between minister and people proved the ruin of many societies. Indeed, such a war as this is a worse calamity than a war with the Indians. That town that maintains a strife with their minister is in a worse condition than that which is infested with cruel savages of the wilderness and cannot go about their work nor lodge in their houses without fear of their lives.

III. If you seek to God that your minister should be a blessing to you, then do what in you lies to encourage his heart and strengthen his hands in his work. Labor to encourage and strengthen by liberally imparting to him of your temporal things, that he may have a comfortable and honorable support and maintenance among you. The great decay of the value of bills of credit does so strangely and invincibly blind many people that it is unspeakably to the injury of the ministry of their Lord, and so without doubt is greatly to the damage and wrong of religion.

If a people have a minister that they see is willing to devote himself to his work and has a disposition to serve his people to his utmost in it, and the people are able, it is wonderful [that is, surprising] that they should be backward plentifully and honorably to support [him] or that they should at all desire that he should be kept low and under difficulties and hardships.

When ministers are kept low and are much straitened in their maintenance, it is a great temptation to them. It tends to dispirit and dishearten them and often proves a temptation to them to neglect their work and is a necessary occasion of their minds being taken up with worldly cares for the support of themselves and families, and so takes off his mind from his proper business and is greatly to the wounding of the souls of the people. And we see that nothing more commonly breeds uneasiness and contention between a minister and people and so overthrows the designs of his ministry than ministers being much straitened for a worldly support.

For a people to be liberal to their minister is the way not only for them to gain in their spiritual interest, but also in their temporal interest. It is [not] the way to lose but greatly to gain and flourish in their estates, as appears by Deuteronomy 14:29, {"And the Levite (because he hath no part nor inheritance with thee), and the stranger, and the fatherless, and the widow, which are within thy gates, shall come, and shall eat and be satisfied; that the Lord thy God may bless thee in all the work of thine hand which thou doest"}; and Malachi 3:10, {"Bring ye all the tithes into the storehouse, that there may be meat in mine house, and prove me now herewith, saith the Lord of hosts, if I will not open you the windows of heaven, and pour you out a blessing, that there shall not be room enough to receive it"}; and

Proverbs 3:9-10, {"Honor the Lord with thy substance, and with the firstfruits of all thine increase: so shall thy barns be filled with plenty, and thy presses shall burst out with new wine"}.

And a people should be careful to strengthen the hands of their minister in another respect, and that is by standing by him in the exercise of church discipline. There is no part of the ministerial work more unfavorable and attended with greater difficulties, and a people may either greatly strengthen or greatly weaken a minister's hands in it. All that have the interest of religion at heart should look upon it [as] their bounden duty to appear and show themselves, or stand by their minister, in the regular exercise of discipline, both that it may be made easy to him and that it may be effectual and successful in its issue. And [they] should say to their minister as the people of Israel said to Ezra the priest concerning his purging out scandal that had crept into the Jewish church: Ezra 10:4, "Arise; for this matter belongeth to thee: we also will be with thee: be of good courage, and do it."

IV. Be ready to submit to your minister in the faithful discharge of his office. Hebrews 13:17, "Obey them that have the rule over you, and submit yourselves: for they watch for your souls, as they that must give account, that they may do it with joy, and not with grief: for that is unprofitable for you." A minister must be faithful to his great Lord and Master, though it should be never so cross to particular men's inclinations, designs, and interests. He must be faithful and thorough in reproving sin, not sparing any through honor or affection or because they are men of estates and influence in the town and so may have power to do him an injury. And what do you set apart this day for but to pray that he may be faithful and that he may be blessed in that faithfulness? And therefore do not oppose him in this faithfulness, however cross it may be in some instance to your practices or carnal interests.

Almost everyone loves a good minister in the general notion. If they should be inquired of what minister they should choose, [they] would readily make answer: a good, faithful minister, one that loves God and will be thorough in his work. But there are many that cannot bear such a minister in the application and experiment. They would have him faithful to others, but they cannot bear that he should deal faithfully with them. They love a faithful minister at a distance only.

But seeing you have set apart this day to fast and pray to God that your minister you are about to settle may be faithful and be successful in that way, let none hereafter be so inconsistent with themselves as by those means or any other to oppose his faithfulness or prevent his successfulness, but let your profession and practice agree together. As you profess and desire of God's blessing in this affair, so let there be consequent the use of all proper means to that end.

NOTES

1   *Boston News-Letter*, quoted in Sylvester Judd, *The History of Hadley, Massachusetts* (1905; reprint, Somersworth, NH: New Hampshire Publishing Company, 1976), 322.

2   For more on Edward Billing, see "Ministers to Preach Not Their Own Wisdom but the Word of God" and "The Work of the Ministry Is Saving Sinners" in this volume.

3   Quoted in Judd, *The History of Hadley, Massachusetts*, 321.

8

EDITORS' INTRODUCTION

PREACHING THE GOSPEL
BRINGS POOR SINNERS
TO CHRIST

Following his dismissal from the Northampton church on June 22, 1750, Edwards remained in the town for over a year, often filling the pulpit of the church formerly under his charge. In 1751 he accepted an offer to become a missionary to the Native Americans at the frontier town of Stockbridge, Massachusetts. On August 8 of that year, he was installed as both missionary to the Stockbridge Indians and pastor of the town's small church. For the fast preceding the occasion, he preached this sermon to the Mohicans and Mohawks living at Stockbridge, urging them to receive the salvation that the Gospel proclaimed.

In this sermon Edwards states that the Gospel is the exclusive way of the salvation of sinners. Persons who know nothing of Christ cannot be saved, for "how shall they receive him into their hearts, believe in him, and love him" if they have not heard of him? "Though there be a way to heaven, yet how shall men go there if they do not know the way?" For this reason Edwards promoted missionary activity and took a keen interest especially in preaching the

Gospel to Native Americans. "The preaching of the Gospel is the means God has provided for bringing poor sinners to Christ and salvation by him."[1]

Edwards's manuscript for this sermon is in the briefer outline form that he adopted in the 1740s. He wrote this on varying sizes of paper, consistent with his habit of using whatever paper he had at hand.[2]

———

The manuscript, held by the Beinecke Rare Book and Manuscript Library, Yale University, consists of a total of four leaves, two octavo and two duodecimo. At the top of the left-hand column on the first page, Edwards wrote, "Fast before installment. Stock[bridge] Ind[ians] and Mohawks Aug[ust] 1751."

PREACHING THE GOSPEL
BRINGS POOR SINNERS
TO CHRIST

ACTS 16:9

And a vision appeared to Paul in the night; There stood a man of Macedonia, and prayed him, saying, Come over into Macedonia, and help us.

Macedonia was a country where the people were ignorant and had not had the Gospel preached to them. The apostle Paul was now traveling to preach the Gospel to those that were ignorant and had hitherto lived in darkness. And he now lodged in a place that was where there was part of the sea between him and Macedonia. And it being the will of God that he should go over into Macedonia and instruct the people there, God caused this vision to appear to him of a man of that country standing and praying.[3]

This shows:

I. What great need poor sinners, as they are by nature, stand in of help;

II. And that there is help provided for poor sinners by Jesus Christ;

III. Particularly, how such as live without the Gospel are in a sorrowful case and stand in great need of help;

IV. And that this help is to be obtained by the preaching of the Gospel.

I. The text shows [man] is in a very miserable state and condition. [He] lost the favor of God, lost eternal life, lost all. [Man] is a poor lost creature. [He] is a poor miserable captive in the hands of Satan. [Man] is a poor prisoner condemned to eternal destruction. [He] is sick with a very terrible and mortal disease, like one that is bitten by a serpent that is full of deadly poison. In this state, [man] could not help himself. [He] had no strength of his own. [He] was poor and had no money. [He] had no wisdom. No creature could help. Men could not help one another. None of the angels [could help].

II. There is help provided for poor, lost sinners in Jesus Christ. When we were helpless, the only begotten Son of God undertook [our help]. When he saw our miserable case, he pitied [us]. He was sufficient for our help, though none was found sufficient. {He was} wise enough, strong enough, worthy and excellent enough. He came into the world and took on him the nature of man. He laid down his life, shed his own precious blood, [and] thereby made full satisfaction for our sins. [He] paid a sufficient price to pay all the debt we owed to God. [He paid] a price sufficient to purchase heaven. He is ascended into heaven and is appointed of God to rule over the whole world. And he is able to bestow that salvation on sinners that he has purchased by his obedience and sufferings. [He is] able to overcome the devil and all the enemies of our souls.

[God is] able to open our eyes and give us new hearts, able to bring all his people that trust in him to heaven, able to make them perfectly holy in heaven, able to raise up their bodies at the end of the world, [and] make both soul and body happy and glorious to all eternity.

III. Still, they that live without the Gospel are in a sorrowful case and greatly need help. Though there be help provided, they know nothing of it. Though there be a Savior, yet if they do not [know] anything of him, how shall they take any care to get an interest in him? If they know nothing of Christ, how shall they receive him into their hearts, believe in him, and love him? How shall they come to Christ for salvation? Though there be a way to heaven, yet how shall men go there if they do not know the way?

IV. Help is provided for the ignorant by the preaching of the Gospel. [The] Gospel declares and makes known the Savior, shows his excellency and glory, tells how great his love is, what he has done and suffered for poor sinners. [The Gospel tells] what we must do. The preaching of the Gospel is the means God has provided for bringing poor sinners to Christ and salvation by him. It is in this way [that] God gives his Spirit to sanctify men.

APPLICATION

I. This may teach you how great your calamity was before you had the Gospel preached and what cause [you have] of thankfulness. There is no other savior for any of mankind. The Gospel is the means God has provided for all nations.

II. We hence see that when a people have formerly had a minister to preach the Gospel to them and he is taken away by death and they are left destitute, they greatly need help. When a people are destitute of a minister to preach the Gospel to them, they are often in a very sorrowful case. The devil often gets many advantages, and things run into great confusion. Darkness and wickedness increase. This has been your case.[4]

III. How much to blame they are that do not care for the Gospel, that neglect it and will not make improvement of it when they have it, will not hearken to ministers. If men will not hearken, [the Gospel will] do them no good, but hurt.

IV. What cause there is for you to pray earnestly to God for his blessing, now that you are about to settle a minister to preach the Gospel to you. A people need God's blessing in this affair above all others, for this is what their good and welfare more depends on than any other. Though the preaching of the Gospel be an excellent means, very suitable for your help, yet it will do nothing without God's blessing with it. You had need [that is, ought] to pray for God's blessing on the minister, that he may have wisdom and grace, and that God will assist him in his work. The work of the ministry is a very great work, attended with a great many difficulties. The devil tries to hinder ministers all that ever he can.

You had need [that is, ought] to pray for God's blessing on you, that you may hearken to [the preaching of the Gospel] and that you may receive saving good. Unless God gives his Spirit, all will be in vain. Consider how much your happiness and the happiness of your children [depends upon God's blessing]. If God gives his blessing, it will tend to your being a truly happy people, happy in this world and that which is to come.

If the work of the ministry is blessed among you, you will not only be happy yourself, but it will have a tendency to the good of other Indians. When they see the good effects, it will make them entertain high and honorable thoughts of religion and dispose them also to seek after instruction.

Therefore, this day, all set yourselves and put away all your sins from you. For God will not hear the prayers of such as go on in their wickedness. And if you go on in drunkenness and other wickedness, the Gospel will be in vain. You will be the devil's people and will go to hell notwithstanding. And you will have a worse place in hell than those that never heard the Gospel preached.

NOTES

1   For discussion of Edwards's understanding of non-Christian religions, see Gerald R. McDermott, *Jonathan Edwards Confronts the Gods: Christian Theology, Enlightenment Religion, and Non-Christian Faiths* (New York: Oxford University Press, 2000).

2   For a discussion of Edwards's shift from "full" manuscripts to outlined manuscripts, see Kenneth P. Minkema, "Preface to the Period," in Edwards, *Sermons and Discourses, 1723-1729,* ed. Minkema, Vol. 14 of *Works of Jonathan Edwards* (New Haven, CT: Yale University Press, 1997), 12-13.

3   Edwards deleted with a diagonal line: "This shows how men that live in darkness and have not the gospel preached to them greatly need help."

4   Here Edwards referred to the loss of the town's previous missionary, John Sergeant, who died in 1749. Edwards succeeded him. See Iain H. Murray, *Jonathan Edwards: A New Biography* (Carlisle, PA: Banner of Truth, 1987), 358.

9

EDITORS' INTRODUCTION

THE WORK OF THE MINISTRY IS SAVING SINNERS

This is the second ordination sermon that Edwards preached for Edward Billing. He and Billing had maintained their friendship since the first one on May 7, 1740. The Communion controversy that Edwards precipitated in Northampton in 1749 divided the ministers of Hampshire County. Billing supported Edwards, but his Cold Spring church refused to appoint him to the council investigating the controversy. Billing nevertheless attended the council as an observer and threw his influence behind Edwards. In the end, however, his support was not enough. The council voted against Edwards by a margin of five to four.[1]

Afterward Billing continued to support Edwards's cause. In 1752 he published *A Dialogue on the Christian Sacraments*, in which he espoused the same views as Edwards. Like the Northampton church, the Cold Spring church dismissed Billing.[2] Two years later he accepted a call from the newly formed church at Greenfield, Massachusetts, and again asked Edwards to preach the installation sermon. Billing was installed on March 28, 1754, and served there until his death in 1760.[3] In this sermon, his last extant sermon devoted to the ministerial cause, Edwards reminded his friend to imitate Christ, who expended himself for the salvation and happiness of sinners. So ministers ought to deny themselves and labor for the salvation of sinners.

Edwards broke from his usual method and omitted the "Application." This possibly occurred due to the special nature of the occasion, but this seems unlikely since his other ministerial sermons included an application. Since he had preached this passage in 1745, perhaps he borrowed the application from an earlier sermon without noting it.[4] It is also possible that he either did not write out this portion, planning to apply the doctrine extemporaneously, or that he skipped it altogether due to the extended length of his sermon.

The manuscript, held by the Beinecke Rare Book and Manuscript Library, Yale University, consists of twenty-eight duodecimo leaves. On the first page, at the top of the left-hand column, Edwards wrote, "Prepared for the installment of Mr. Billing on March 28, 1754. Preached also at No. 3 July, 1756 at Mr. Jones' ordination."[5]

THE WORK OF THE MINISTRY
IS SAVING SINNERS

ACTS 20:28

Take heed therefore unto yourselves, and to all the flock, over which the Holy Ghost has made you overseers, to feed the church of God, which he hath purchased with his own blood.

These are the words of the apostle Paul to the elders of the church of Ephesus, one of the greatest cities of the Roman Empire. This apostle was the great Apostle of the Gentiles, and one that was made the greatest instrument of propagating, enlarging, and building up the kingdom of Christ and saving the souls of men by far of all the ministers of Christ that ever were. It is owing to him chiefly under Christ that the nations of Europe and most other nations that profess the Christian religion are at this day any other than pagans and gross idolaters, as they all formerly were.

And of all the places where the apostle preached the Gospel, there is none where he seems to have had such great success as at Ephesus. There were two distinct times of his preaching the Gospel in that city. First was in his return from Greece, the first time that ever he went into Europe, when he was on his way from Corinth to Jerusalem, at which time he made but a very short stay there. We have an account of it in Acts 18:19-21: "And he came to Ephesus, and left them there: but he himself entered into the synagogue, and reasoned with the Jews. When they desired him to tarry longer time with them, he consented not; but bade them farewell, saying, I must by all means keep this feast that cometh in Jerusalem: but I will return again unto you, if God will. And he sailed from Ephesus." The other time was after his return from Jerusalem, when he labored in Ephesus a long time, continuing there by the space of three years, as [says] verse 31 of the context [Acts 20]. We have an account of his labors and great success there at that time in the nineteenth chapter of Acts. We are told, verses 19-21, "Many of them also which used curious arts brought their books together, and burned them before all men: and they counted the price of them, and found it fifty thousand pieces of silver. So mightily grew the word of God and prevailed. After these things were ended, Paul purposed in the spirit, when he had passed through Macedonia and Achaia, to go to Jerusalem, saying, After I have been there, I must also see Rome."

We have an account in the chapter wherein is my text how the apostle, again in his second return from Greece to Jerusalem, came near the city of Ephesus but did not go into the city lest he should be hindered on his voyage, but sent for the elders of the church to come to him to Miletus, where he had this discourse with those elders, of which the text is a part. Probably some others of his Christian friends came forth with those elders to see their dear spiritual father, of whom the apostle takes a most affectionate leave, as never expecting to see them again in this world, verse 25. But he directs his speech especially to the elders of the church, with whom he leaves his parting charge in the text.

1. The work or business that he charges them to perform.

2. What part of the church of God were to be the more special subjects of their care and labors in this great work.

3. Why they ought in a special manner to take care of the spiritual welfare of this part. [The] Holy Ghost had made them overseers.

4. After what manner they are directed to attend this business and perform this work.

5. What they were to have an eye to in a special manner to influence and direct them in this great work.

DOCTRINE

My design from these words is to consider Christ's expending his own blood for the salvation and happiness of the souls of men, in the view both of an inducement and a direction to ministers to exert themselves for the same end.

The method in which I shall by divine help prosecute this design is:

I. To observe what there is in Christ's shedding his blood for the salvation and happiness of the souls of men that should be regarded by ministers as an inducement to exert themselves for the same end.

II. How Christ's shedding his blood {for the salvation and happiness of the souls of men} should be regarded by ministers for their direction as to the manner in which they should seek {to exert themselves for the same end}.

III. Observe some special reasons why Christ's shedding his blood for {the salvation and happiness of the souls of men} should thus be regarded by ministers to induce and direct them in exerting themselves for the same end.

IV. Conclude with some consideration for the enforcement of the whole.

I. The first thing is to observe {what there is in Christ's shedding his blood for the salvation and happiness of the souls of men that should be regarded by ministers as an inducement to exert themselves for the same end}. And here are the following things worthy to be considered concerning this: first, the nature and manner of this wonderful act or behavior of Christ, his expending his blood; second, the person whose blood was shed; third, the end for which he shed his blood; fourth, the things which appear and are manifested by it.

First. The nature and manner of this wonderful act or behavior of Christ in shedding his blood is worthy to be considered as an inducement to ministers to exert themselves for the good of souls. I speak of Christ's shedding his blood not merely as an event or a thing wherein he was passive, but {wherein he was active}. John 10:17-18, "Therefore does my Father love {me}, because I lay down my life, that I might take it again. No man taketh it from me, but I lay it down of myself. I have power to lay it down, and I have power to take it again. This commandment have I received of my Father."

Now concerning the nature of this act or conduct of Christ, if we consider it, we may observe how greatly Christ exerted or laid out himself therein for the good of the souls of men. Christ did much for the souls of men of old in the revelations he made of himself in coming down from heaven and manifesting himself in visible symbols of his presence, appearing as he did. He did much for the good of men's souls in the words which he spoke in the manifold revelations which he made of himself in so many instructions, counsels, directions, and warnings as he gave. {He did much for the good of men's souls in} speaking from Mt. Sinai, {in} writing his law on tables of stone, {in} commanding {his law} to be written in a book, {in} sending so many prophets. He did great things {for the good of men's souls} in the miracles which he wrought of old.

But Christ did all these things without any labor, trouble, or expense. Indeed, God represents him as appearing as one that was zealous, diligent, and earnestly engaged, rising early and sending them. But yet in these there was truly no painful endeavor or effort, no degree of suffering or proper self-denial. {He did all these things} with perfect ease. But when Christ became incarnate, he immediately began a life and labor [of] difficulty and sorrow. He went through a course of hard labors for the salvation and happiness of the souls of men when he went about doing good, laboring in prayer, in preaching the everlasting Gospel everywhere and to all sorts of person[s] not only on sabbath days but from day to day, and healing the sick, casting out devils. Laboring thus not only on sabbath days but from day to day, both day and night, in much travail, in poverty, hunger, thirst, in weariness, in reproach and continual persecution of his enemies.

His life was a life of sore conflict with the enemies of the souls of men, which he engaged and continued in for their salvation.

And in the conclusion of these labors and this conflict, he suffered to the utmost extremity. So great was the labor and wrestling of his soul, so great his sorrow and agony the evening before his crucifixion, that his sweat was as it were great drops of blood falling down to the ground, which was occasioned only by a clear view and expectation of what he was [to] undergo the next day on the cross.

If the very sight of the cup that he was to drink put his human nature into such an agony, how bitter indeed was the cup itself when he came to drink it, and even the very dregs of it, while he was hanging six hours on the cross in the most extreme lingering torments of body and under that darkness and shadow of death on his soul, which he suffered when he cried out, "My God, my God why hast thou forsaken me?"

Then he paid a great price indeed for the salvation and happiness of the souls of men. Extreme were the labors he then underwent. Terrible was the conflict he then had with his strong and cruel enemies, and great was the expense, when he expended this which is of all things dearest to human nature, even his blood, his life, and his soul, when he poured out his soul unto death; yea, gave himself in both body and soul [as] an offering for sin and as the price of the eternal happiness of the souls of men as it were in a furnace, and that the most terrible, the furnace of the holy wrath and vengeance of God for the sins of man.

He did not die a natural but a violent death, and that not an accidental death, but he was executed as a malefactor and suffered that kind of execution that of all that was then in use in the world was the most painful and the most ignominious, wherein he suffered the most extreme degree of the contempt and cruelty of the vilest and worst of men, and of all ranks of men and of devils; and, which was more than all, he suffered the terrible effects of the holy wrath of God.

Second. Another thing worthy to be considered to induce ministers to exert themselves for the good of souls is the person that thus shed his blood for them. Not only the nature of what was done and suffered in shedding blood for the souls of men should be considered, but also whose blood it was that was shed. And we are told in the text that it was the blood of God. "Feed the church of God, which he hath purchased with his own blood." The person that shed his blood was a divine person, being not only man but God. And it being so that that blood was the blood of God, the following things are here worthy to be remarked:

1. That it was the blood of one of infinite dignity and glory, and so was blood that was infinitely precious. And what was done in shedding of it for sinners was a thing infinitely great, infinitely greater than if the greatest earthly potentate had shed his blood, or than if all the princes on earth {had shed their blood}; yea, an infinitely greater {thing than if} the highest created angel {had shed his blood}; yea, and not only so, but an infinitely greater thing than if the whole glorious host of those pure and glorious spirits {had shed their blood}.

In that it was the blood of God, it was the blood of him before whom all the kings of the earth are as grasshoppers, and the blood of one that was the great Creator and King of angels. He by whom, as the apostle observes in Colossians 1:16-17, "all things were created, that are in heaven, and that are in earth, visible and invisible, whether they be thrones, or dominions, or principalities, or powers: by whom and from whom all things were created: and who is before all things, and by whom all things consist."

2. In that it was God's own blood, it was the blood of one that had been from all eternity infinitely happy. As it is a greater thing for one that is great and honorable to suffer than for another that is meaner [that is, more common], so it is a greater thing for one that is originally in a very happy state to be willing to descend into a state of affliction and torment than another. The self-denial in it is greater in proportion to the degree of happiness he descends from.

It is a harder thing for one that at present is not only at ease but in very prosperous and joyful circumstances to comply to come down from such a state, in circumstances of extreme calamity and sorrow, than for another whose original circumstances are already not very prosperous and not at so great a remove from the suffering which is proposed.

When Christ was on earth, his human soul had communicated to it a kind of memory or consciousness of the happiness which his person had with God the Father before the world was, as far as a human mind was capable of it. And he reflected on this when he was going to shed his blood, as appears by what he says in the prayer he made the night before his crucifixion, John 17:5: "And now, O Father, glorify thou me with thine own self with the glory which I had with thee before the world was." So that he had that happiness which he had with his Father from eternity to compare with the extreme sufferings that there were set before his eyes, which makes the self-denial infinitely greater than it otherwise would have been. In order rightly to judge of the degrees of Christ's self-denial for the salvation of souls, we must take our measure from the height of happiness he was in before to the depth of sorrow, pain, and contempt he descended to from there. And this will show it to be immeasurable, incomprehensible, and surely[6] infinitely great.

It is to be considered that the happiness that Christ had before the world was consisted in the enjoyment of his Father's love, so that he knew by experience the infinite value of that love, which made it infinitely harder to him to have the comforts of that love withdrawn by God's departing and hiding himself from him as he did on the cross, and when he in some sort suffered the Father's wrath at that time when he cried out, "My God, My God, why hast thou forsaken me?"

3. In that it was God's own blood, it was the blood of one that was infinitely above any need of us. Christ, as he was God, was infinitely above any need of anything. God is self-sufficient. His happiness is in himself. As his being is necessary and underived, so is his happiness and glory. It is underived as to any cause or author. No other being is the author of [it]. It is underived as to the fountain and object in the enjoyment of which he is happy, {that is,} enjoyment of himself.

Indeed, the eternal, infinite happiness of the Divine Being seems to be social, consisting in the infinitely blessed union and society of the persons of the Trinity, so that they are happy in one another. So God the Father and God the Son are represented as rejoicing from eternity one in another, Proverbs 8:30: "Then was I by him, as one brought up with him: and I was daily his delight, rejoicing always before him."

So that, according to our imperfect way of conceiving and speaking of things, the persons of the Trinity gave one another happiness, or derived happiness one from another. But this argues no dependence on any other being. On the contrary, it shows God's absolute independence on [that is, of] the creature. As Christ is infinitely happy in the bosom of the Father, he is independent on [that is, of] us and stands in no need of us, and so stands in no need of our redemption and salvation. As Christ's blood was the blood of God, so it was the blood of one that could not stand in need of us, because he was omnipotent.

It being thus, it is evident that he that shed his blood for sinners needed not our salvation. Our sin and misery could not hurt him, nor did he need that we should be made holy and happy. He needs not our presence with him in heaven, nor can he be profited by anything that we can be or do there.

4. In that it was God's own blood that was shed for sinners, it was the blood of one that [is] infinitely above all possibility of being requited for shedding his own blood. This also appears by what has been already observed of God's self-sufficiency and Christ's infinite happiness in the bosom of the Father. The happiness that is infinite cannot be added to.

In that Christ was God, it appears that he is above all capacity of being requited, {because he is} immutable.

In that he is God, he cannot be profited by us, because he is one on whom we are universally and absolutely dependent, {and from whom we} derive all.

In that it was God's own blood that was shed, it is further evident that it is utterly impossible that we should ever requite him for such a benefit, the benefit is so great. If it had been possible that we should requite him for some instances of his kindness, which it is not, yet it would be utterly impossible. These things which manifest the love, adoration, and praises of the redeemed do nothing to requite or make compensation for {such a benefit}.

How high soever their love may be raised, how ardent soever their flame may be, in how pure and excellent a manner soever; how exalted soever their praises may be, and how many soever may be united, and how long soever their love and praises may be continued; yea, and though the whole glorious assembly should be increasing, [they] never could do anything towards making a requital.

5. In that the blood that was shed for the souls of men was the blood of God, it was the blood of one to whom those that it was shed for are enemies. Sinners are enemies to God. The very nature of sin is enmity against God. The very notion of sin is opposition or contrariety to God, opposition to his will, as expressed in his law. 1 John 3:4, "Sin is the transgression of the law."

As sin is an opposition to the law of God and rebellion against the Lawgiver, so it is an opposing [of] the authority of God and a contempt of his infinite majesty.

And as it is an opposition to the holy will of God, so it is a contrariety and enmity against the nature of God. For his will [is] but an expression of his holy nature, which is infinitely contrary to sin. By his holy nature he is of "purer eyes than to behold evil and cannot look on iniquity" [Habakkuk 1:13].

And as sin is an opposition to God's nature, so it implies a contrariety to all his perfections. For the nature of God and his perfections are not different. And in being an opposition to his perfections, so it is an opposition to his life and essence and very being. For the being of God and the being of his nature and perfections cannot be distinguished.

And as sin is an opposition to the nature of God, so it is an opposition to his works. It is opposing the design of God in the creation of the world, which was his own glory and the spiritual and eternal excellency and happiness of his creatures. It is particularly contrary to the work of God in the creation of man, especially in that wherein man's essence mainly consists as distinguished from inferior creatures, namely, understanding and reason. Sin is contrary to reason and so a violation of the law of nature, which is the law of reason. And it is an opposition to the special end of God in his creation of man, which is that he might glorify God actively.

The very nature of sin is enmity against God. Sin in its principle and habit is nothing else but a habitual or natural enmity against

God. Romans 8:7, "The carnal mind [is enmity against God: for it is not subject to the law of God, neither indeed can be]." And sin, in its acts, is a militating [or] fighting against God and walking contrary to him. Leviticus 26:21, "And if ye walk contrary unto me, and will not hearken unto me; I will bring seven times more plagues upon you according to your sins." So in verses 23 and 27 and other parts of the chapter. Acts 5:39, "Lest we be found fighting against God." 1 Corinthians 10:22, "Do we provoke the Lord to jealousy?"

And as Christ, therefore, who shed his blood for sinners, is a divine person or God as well as man, he shed his blood for his enemies. Romans 5:8, "while we were yet sinners, Christ died for us," and verse 10, "if, when we were enemies, we were reconciled to God by the death of his Son."

Not only for such as had no worthiness, no beauty to attract, but those who were altogether unworthy, filthy, odious, ill deserving. And not only so, but those whose odiousness and unworthiness consisted especially in a direct enmity and opposition to himself, which is what makes his so exerting himself and giving himself for their happiness peculiarly wonderful.

And here it is worthy to be observed that as the very nature of sin consists in enmity to Christ, as he was a divine person, so this nature of it never so remarkably and clearly appeared as at that very time when {he} shed his blood {for his enemies}, and in some of those very persons for whom that blood was shed and that were to be saved by it.

6. In that the blood that Christ shed was the blood of God, it was the blood [of one] that was perfectly knowing of all the unworthiness of those that he died for. He is an omniscient Being. He is acquainted with every individual sinner all over the world and in all ages, and he perfectly knows all their sins of heart, lip, and life. We see but a little of the wickedness that is committed around us, but God sees it all. He sees all that is done in secret, {all that is done} in darkness or light, {all that is done} at midnight. Roofs and walls are no coverings. Yea, he searches the heart. {He sees} all that wickedness that is in the hearts of men. This is peculiar to the Divine Being. Amos 4:13, [he] "declares

unto man what is his thought." But Christ has this prerogative. John 2:24-25, "he knew all men, and needed not that any should testify of man: for he knew what was in man." And then Christ as God perfectly saw and understood all that evil that is in sin, which cannot be comprehended by any man or angel because it is infinite.

That he should shed his blood for sinners was on this account more wonderful, in that he not only suffered such great things for those that were so unworthy, but that as having perfect view of all the sins of the whole world and of all the odiousness, vileness, and ill desert that there is in sin.

Third. Another thing worthy to be considered by ministers to induce them to exert themselves for the good of souls is the end for which so great a person shed his blood, that we are told in the text was that he might purchase those that he died [for]. He shed his blood to purchase the souls of men. This implies two things that Christ aimed at by it, namely, that they might be his and that he might save them. These may be considered distinctly as distinct motives to ministers to exert themselves for the good of the souls of men.

1. The special relation and peculiar union of the souls of men to himself that Christ aimed at in shedding his blood. When a man purchases any thing, he pays a price for it that it may be his. So Christ shed his blood and gave his life as a price to purchase the souls of men, that they might be his in a manner they were not his before—not as all things in heaven and earth are his, not as wicked men and devils are his, and as the souls of men are his prior to their redemption, but that they may be his in a new manner, in a special propriety, relation, and a peculiar union and use. Though all things in heaven and earth are Christ's, yet the saints are his in a peculiar and distinguished manner. [They are] his part, [his] firstfruits, his chosen people, [his] peculiar people, [his] peculiar treasure, [his] peculiar propriety. [They have a special] relation and union, [a special] use.

2. Another thing which Christ aimed at in shedding his blood for the souls of men, implied in his doing it to purchase them, is the salvation that they are the subjects of through their special relation and union to him. Purchasing is a phrase that implies as much as redeem-

ing in Scripture, but redemption implies salvation. Therefore, ministers should consider the greatness of that salvation that Christ shed his blood to procure for the souls of men, to excite them to labor for their good.

(1) The greatness of the misery that he died to save them from.

(2) The greatness of the happiness he gave the price of his blood to procure. For Christ's blood is not only a propitiation for sin, a satisfactory price to save from hell, but it is also to be considered as the price of happiness and glory. If it be considered with regard to what he suffered in it, {it is} a propitiation. So with regard [to] what he did, or viewing it as a voluntary offering, [it is] positively meritorious.

Now the exceeding greatness of the glory and happiness which Christ died to purchase for the souls of men may well move them to exert themselves that they may be brought to this happiness, [to an] inheritance incorruptible, [a] crown of glory, [to] reign with Christ [and] partake with him. I know of no greater argument of the exceeding greatness of the happiness and glory {which Christ died to purchase} than the greatness of the price {and} the excellency of that righteousness.

Fourth. Another thing which should be considered in Christ's shedding his blood and undergoing such extreme sufferings for the souls of men is what was manifested thereby. Here I shall mention two things in particular.

1. The great regard that Christ hereby manifested to that honor and glory of God which is promoted by such a salvation and happiness of souls.

What Christ did and suffered in the work of our redemption was done and suffered from love to God and a regard to his will and glory, as is very manifest. John 12:27-28, "Now is my soul troubled; and what shall I say? Father, save me from this hour: but for this cause came I unto this hour. Father, glorify thy name." Ephesians 1:6-7, "To the praise and glory of his grace, wherein he hath made us accepted in the beloved. In whom we have redemption through his blood, the forgiveness of sins, according to the riches of his grace."

Christ manifested an infinite regard to the glory of God in dying for sinners in many respects. It showed an infinite regard to the honor of God's majesty, authority, and holy love that when he loved men and desired their salvation, he was willing [to die for sinners]. It showed an infinite regard to the will or the command of God. For the laying down [of] his life was, as it were, an infinite trial of his obedience. Psalm 40:7-8, "Then said I, Lo, I come: in the volume of the book it is written of me, I delight to do thy will, O my God: yea, thy law is within my heart." Isaiah 50:5-6, "The Lord hath opened mine ear, and I was not rebellious, neither turned away back. I gave my back to the smiters, and my cheeks to them that plucked off the hair: I hid not my face from shame and spitting." And it showed a regard to the glory {of God}, as all God's perfections have their most glorious display in the way of salvation.

Seeing Christ manifested so great a regard to the honor of God in the salvation of souls, surely his ministers ought earnestly to seek that they may be the instruments of promoting of the glory of God in the same thing.

That Christ should have such a regard {to the honor of God in the salvation of souls} is a bright and most affecting manifestation of the infinite value of God's honor and glory, and so its worthiness [is] to be earnestly sought by ministers of the Gospel.

2. Another thing that was manifest by Christ's shedding his blood {and undergoing such extreme sufferings} was his great love to the souls and his infinite regard to their welfare. This is many ways most clearly and wonderfully manifest by things which have already been [mentioned]. The nature of Christ's sufferings manifest [his worthiness]. And that they were the sufferings of such a person, [they were the] sufferings of one who knew his own dignity. {And that they were the sufferings of such a person, they were the} sufferings of one that was so happy, {the sufferings of} one so disinterested. {And that they were the sufferings of such a person, they were} for those that were so unworthy enemies. {And that they were the sufferings of such a person, they were the sufferings of} one who had all the sinful and all the infinite deformity of it in his comprehensive and

absolutely perfect view. The end for which [was] to bring to such a union, so great benefit in consequence.

Now Christ so loved the souls of men, and had so great a regard to their salvation, that he thought it worthy for him so to lay out himself. Shall not his ministers and servants be willing {to do the same}? In how clear and striking a manner does what Christ has done and suffered demonstrate the worth of the souls of men. If Christ thought the worth of souls to be so great as to answer such labors, such suffering, shall ministers begrudge Christ the same?

Thus I have considered Christ's shedding his blood for the salvation and happiness of the souls of men as an inducement to ministers to exert themselves for the same end.

I now proceed, [in the]

II. Second place, to observe how Christ's shedding his blood for the salvation and happiness of souls should be regarded by ministers for the direction as to the manner in which they ought to seek the same. And here are three things belonging to Christ's shedding his blood that ministers ought to look at for their direction in this matter: first, the thing itself that Christ did in voluntarily thus shedding {his blood for the salvation and happiness of souls}; second, the manner and circumstance of doing this; third, the virtues exercised in doing it.

First. The thing itself that Christ did in shedding {his blood for the salvation and happiness of souls} should be regarded by ministers as their example and direction. If Christ so loved the souls of men as to lay out himself and deny himself at this rate for the salvation {and happiness of souls}, then surely the ministers of Christ should be ready greatly to exert themselves and deny themselves and suffer for the sake {of the salvation and happiness of souls}. For as Christ often said, "The servant is not above his master, nor the disciple above his lord" {Matthew 10:24}.

When Christ was giving his parting charges to his disciples the very evening before his crucifixion, he gave this as, in a peculiar and eminent manner, his commandment, {that they} should love one another as he loved them. John 15:12, "This is my commandment,

That ye love one another, as I have loved you." We may see in what respect Christ means that they should {love one another} by what follows in the next verse, "Greater love hath no man than this, that a man lay down his life for his friends."

An imitation of Christ in laying down his life for the good of souls is in Scripture in a peculiar manner recommended to ministers. Matthew 20:26-28, "Whosoever will be great among you, let him be your minister; and he that will be chief among you, let him be your servant: even as the Son of man came not to be ministered unto, but to minister, and to give his life a ransom for many." And this is undoubtedly the chief design of what Christ did and said to his disciples that we have an account of, John 13:4-16,

> [*He riseth from supper, and laid aside his garments; and took a towel, and girded himself. After that he poureth water into a basin, and began to wash the disciples' feet, and to wipe them with the towel wherewith he was girded. Then cometh he to Simon Peter: and Peter saith unto him, Lord, dost thou wash my feet? Jesus answered and said unto him, What I do thou knowest not now; but thou shalt know hereafter. Peter saith unto him, Thou shalt never wash my feet. Jesus answered him, If I wash thee not, thou hast no part with me. Simon Peter saith unto him, Lord, not my feet only, but also my hands and my head. Jesus saith to him, He that is washed needeth not save to wash his feet, but is clean every whit: and ye are clean, but not all. For he knew who should betray him; therefore said he, Ye are not all clean. So after he had washed their feet, and had taken his garments, and was set down again, he said unto them, Know ye what I have done to you? Ye call me Master and Lord: and ye say well; for so I am. If I, then, your Lord and Master, have washed your feet; ye also ought to wash one another's feet. For I have given you an example, that ye should do as I have done to you. Verily, verily, I say unto you, The servant is not greater than his lord; neither he that is sent greater than he that sent him.*]

What the duty is that Christ intended is explained by the practice of the apostle, which he speaks of, 1 Corinthians 9:19: "For though I be free from all men, yet have I made myself servant unto all, that I might gain the more." So this seems manifestly Christ's meaning in what he says to Peter after his resurrection, John 21:17-19:

> He saith unto him the third time, Simon, son of Jonas, lovest thou me? Peter was grieved because he said unto him the third time, Lovest thou me? And he said unto him, Lord, thou knowest all things; thou knowest that I love thee. Jesus saith unto him, Feed my sheep. Verily, verily, I say unto thee, When thou wast young, thou girdedst thyself, and walkedst whither thou wouldest: but when thou shalt be old, thou shalt stretch forth thy hands, and another shall gird thee, and carry thee whither thou wouldest not. This spake he, signifying by what death he should glorify God. And when he had spoken this, he saith unto him, Follow me.

Upon the hearing [of] these things, some may possibly be ready to object and say, "What, is it the duty of ministers to shed their blood for the souls of men as Christ did?" I answer: Though there be no need of any further propitiation, and though it be great impiety in any to go about to offer to God {to shed their blood for the souls of men as Christ did} under any such notion, yet it is undoubtedly the duty of ministers to be ready for the greatest condescension and abasement of themselves, and to be of that spirit to be willing to deny themselves even to the utmost as to all temporal things, and even of their own lives, if they should be called to it in divine providence; yea, to undergo the most tormenting and ignominious death, as many of Christ's ministers have been called to it and have actually done it, as the apostles, as we have reason to think, most of them were called to die and seal their testimony. Their practice has best interpreted the rules of this kind which are given ministers in Scripture.

They manifested such a spirit. {They} exposed their lives. Colossians 1:24, "Who now rejoice in my sufferings for you, and fill up that which is behind of the afflictions of Christ in my flesh for his body's sake, which is the church." 2 Corinthians 4:10, "Always bearing about in the body the dying of the Lord Jesus, that the life also of Jesus might be made manifest in our body."

The apostle speaks of it as the duty of Christians in general. 1 John 3:16, "Hereby perceive we the love of God, because he laid down his life for us: and we ought to lay down our lives for the brethren." But especially is it the duty of ministers. The apostle instructs Timothy that as ministers would acquit themselves as good soldiers of Jesus Christ, they should be ready to deny themselves of all the enjoyments of this life. 2 Timothy 2:3-4, "Thou therefore endure hardness, as a good soldier of Jesus Christ. No man that warreth entangleth himself with the affairs of this life; that he may please him who hath chosen him to be a soldier." And as "Christ loved the church and gave himself for it, that he might sanctify and cleanse it with the washing of water by the word" {Ephesians 5:25-26}, so ministers should be ready to give what they have and give themselves, to spend and be spent. 2 Corinthians 12:15, "And I will very gladly spend and be spent."

Second. Another thing that should be regarded by ministers as their example to direct them how they should exert {themselves for the salvation and happiness of souls} was the manner and circumstances with which [Christ] offered up his blood. He did it willingly, not as forced or driven. "No man taketh it from me, I lay it down of myself" [John 10:18]. "Father, glorify thy name" [John 12:28]. Matthew 26:42, "O my Father, if this cup may not pass away from me, except I drink it, thy will be done." He did it with great cheerfulness. Psalm 40:8, "I delight to do thy will, O my God." He could not endure to have anything said against it. Matthew 16:21-23, "From that time forth began Jesus to show unto his disciples, how that he must go unto Jerusalem, and suffer many things of the elders and chief priests and scribes, and be killed, and be raised again the third day. Then Peter took him, and began to rebuke him, saying, Be it far from thee, Lord: this shall not be unto thee. But he turned, and said unto Peter, Get thee behind me, Satan: thou art an offense unto me: for thou savorest not the things that be of God, but those that be of men." John 11:7-8, "He saith unto his disciples, Let us go into Judea again. His disciples say unto him, Master, the Jews of late sought to stone thee; and goest thou thither again?" He went forward towards

Jerusalem as greatly engaged, ascending up to Jerusalem, going before [the Jews again]. He seemed as it were to forget himself in his great concern for the souls of men.

Here is an example for ministers, to teach them with what freedom and alacrity [they should exert themselves], how they should comparatively forget their private interests. Again, he shed his blood for {the salvation and happiness of souls} at a time when he received the worst treatment from those that he shed his blood for. Their ingratitude was at the height. This teaches ministers [how they should exert themselves].

Again, Christ did this in opposition to the greatest temptations of Satan. This should animate and encourage ministers.

Again, Christ offered his own blood, attended with strong agony and tears. Hebrews 5:6-7, "As he saith in another place, Thou art a priest for ever after the order of Melchisedek. Who in the days of his flesh, when he had offered up prayers and supplications with strong crying and tears unto him that was able to save him from death, and was heard in that he feared."

Third. Another thing which ought to be regarded by ministers for their direction in the manner in which they ought {to exert themselves for the salvation and happiness of souls} is the virtues that Christ exercised and manifested in shedding his blood. He died, as has been already observed, in the exercises of a supreme love to God and regard to his honor and glory. Christ's love to his Father had then its greatest trial, and a far greater trial than even the love of other persons, and therefore as his love appeared unconquerable under this trial, it then had its highest manifestation. Christ shed his blood in the exercise of a spirit of filial obedience to his heavenly Father. He did it in the exercise of a holy submission and entire resignation of the will to God.[7] {He did it in the exercise} of the most wonderful patience. He died in the exercise of the greatest humility, of the most wonderful condescension. He condescended greatly in his incarnation. {He died in the exercise} of the most superlative charity and benevolence to mankind, of the most admirable meekness towards his most injurious, spiteful, and contemptuous enemies when they were in the highest exercise of their cruelty and when he was the subject of the most terrible effects of their vile malignity and infinitely horrible contempt. {He died in the exercise of} meekness towards his own disciples when they showed the most ingratitude to him that ever they did.

Here is an example for all the followers of Christ, but more especially an example for ministers, to teach them in what manner they ought to behave themselves in their work. Ministers in the whole course of their labors in the ministry should have a constant regard to the example of Jesus Christ. As Gideon (who undoubtedly was in this very thing designed as a type of Christ), when he went against the great host of the Midianites with his three hundred men with trumpets, lamps, and earthen pitchers. Judges 7:17, "And he said unto them, Look on me, and do likewise: and, behold, when I come to the outside of the camp, it shall be that, and as ye see me do, so shall ye do."

I come now, to the

III. [Third] thing which was at first proposed, to observe some special reasons why Christ's shedding his blood for the salvation and happiness of the souls of men should be regarded by ministers thus to induce and direct them in exerting themselves for the same end. There is much in what Christ did in laying down his life for sinners, and in his conduct under his last sufferings, for the direction of all Christians in their conduct in this world, and much to induce all greatly to exert themselves and to deny themselves and cheerfully to undergo sufferings for the good of others, and especially their spiritual and eternal good, but above all for the inducement and direction of ministers. For the following reasons:

First. Ministers above others have great occasion to have Jesus Christ and what he has done and suffered for souls much in their view. The business of their lives is to contemplate those things and to exhibit to, and [to] enforce them upon others. [A] great part of their business lies in studying the Gospel that exhibits Christ and him crucified, and so it must of necessity be that they must have the person of Christ and his sufferings, with the great ends and circumstances of it and the things manifested by it, continuously as it were before their eye. And as the other great part of their business is to instruct

others in those things and enforce them upon them, this also obliges
them to have them in their own view, with the enforcements of them,
with regard to their own practice and has a peculiar tendency to
impress their minds with them.

Second. The very business to which they are called and directed
is to carry on the design of Christ's death and promote the success of
it in the salvation of souls. Therefore, they are called the ministers of
Christ. They are agents subordinate to him and as ministering to him
and serving him in that great offer of the salvation and happiness of
men's souls. [They] are called coworkers with Christ, 2 Corinthians
6:1: "We then, as workers together with him, beseech you also that
ye receive not the grace of God in vain." The work of the ministry is
the same in many respects as Christ's own work, the work of saving
sinners. 1 Timothy 4:16, "Take heed unto thyself, and unto the doctrine; continue in them: for in doing this thou shall save thyself, and
those that hear thee." James 5:20, "Let him know, that he which con-
verts a sinner from the error of his way shall save a soul from death,
and shall hide a multitude of sins." [They are] called saviors,
Obadiah 21: "And saviors shall come up on mount Zion to judge the
mount of Esau; and the kingdom shall be the Lord's." Christ was a
minister of the Gospel. He was sent forth as the Father's minister, as
the elders of the church are Christ's ministers. John 20:21, "As the
Father hath sent me, so send I you."

Third. Ministers are not only appointed to carry on Christ's work
of saving souls, but as standing in Christ's stead in many respects.
{Ministers stand in Christ's stead as} ambassadors. 2 Corinthians
5:20, "Now then we are ambassadors for Christ, as though God did
beseech you by us: we pray you in Christ's stead, be ye reconciled to
God." [Ministers] speak in his name. [It is] so in administering the
sacraments.

Fourth. The relation of ministers to the church of God is in many
respects an image of that which Christ stands in. Christ is the Great
Shepherd. Christ is the bishop of souls. Christ is God's great prophet
and teacher and the light of the world. Ministers are represented as
light.

Christ is the church's head and ruler. Ministers under Christ are rulers of the church. Hebrews 13:17, "Obey them that have the rule over you." Christ is intercessor. Christ is the spiritual husband. Isaiah 62:5, "For as a young man marrieth a virgin, so shall thy sons marry thee: and as the bridegroom rejoiceth over the bride, so shall thy God rejoice over thee." Christ is the king of angels.

Christ is the great example. Ministers are set to be examples. 1 Peter 5:1-3, "The elders which are among you I exhort, who am also an elder, and a witness of the sufferings of Christ, and also a partaker of the glory that shall be revealed: feed the flock of God which is among you, taking the oversight thereof, not by constraint, but willingly; not for filthy lucre, but of a ready mind; neither as being lords over God's heritage, but being ensamples to the flock." 1 Timothy 4:12, "Let no man despise thy youth; but be thou an example of the believers, in word, in conversation, in charity, in spirit, in faith, in purity."

I come now, in the

IV. [Fourth] and last place, with some additional enforcements of the whole. Here I would briefly suggest these two or three things:

First. Let it be considered that if ministers do exert themselves for the salvation and happiness of the souls of men in imitation of him who has purchased them with his own blood, how excellently and honorably they will be employed. It was greatly in the heart of God to put honor upon his Son, the most honorable and glorious of all God's work. Ministers will have the honor to be coworkers.

Second. Ministers of the Gospel, such as Christ has truly called to that work, may consider to engage themselves to imitate him in what he has done for the salvation of souls, that he has done these things for the salvation of their souls. This is that motive that is intended by Christ, John 13:14: "If I then, your Lord and Master, have washed your feet; ye also ought to wash one another's feet."

Third.[8] As ministers are in a peculiar manner called to do Christ's work, so if they imitate Christ's work they shall in a singular manner be partakers of his reward. Christ, as he is the greatest and most excellent of all the servants of God, is adorned far above all others in his rewards. It is promised to all Christ's faithful followers {that they will} partake with Christ in his rewards, but in a special manner to faithful ministers, those that imitate {Christ}. As their work is greater and {they} are called to greater self-denial, so if {they are faithful, they will have} higher rewards. Christ promised to the first ministers of the Gospel that "when the Son of man shall sit on the throne of his glory, ye also shall sit upon twelve thrones, judging the twelve tribes of Israel" [Matthew 19:28]. The glory of heaven is promised in a peculiar manner to them that are faithful in that great work of turning men to righteousness. Daniel 12:3, "And they that be wise shall shine as the brightness of the firmament; and they that turn many to righteousness as the stars for ever and ever." The apostle tells Timothy for his encouragement to deny himself and suffer in the work of the ministry for the good of souls, that if ministers suffer with Christ, they shall reign with him, mentioning his own example, 2 Timothy 2:8-12: "Remember that Jesus Christ of the seed of David was raised from the dead according to my gospel: wherein I suffer trouble, as an evildoer, even unto bonds; but the word of God is not bound. Therefore I endure all things for the elect's sakes, that they may also obtain the salvation which is in Christ Jesus with eternal glory. It is a faithful saying: For if we be dead with him, we shall also live with him: if we suffer, we shall also reign with him: if we deny him, he also will deny us."

Christ is, as it were, he that has sown the seed in the field. Ministers are sent forth as reapers to gather in the fruits of his labors. And if they are faithful, it is promised that in the end they will rejoice with Christ. John 4:36, "And he that reapeth receiveth wages, and gathereth fruit unto life eternal: that both he that soweth and he that reapeth may rejoice together." The souls that are redeemed by Christ's blood are, as it were, crowns of rejoicing in heaven. Isaiah 62:5, "For as a young man marrieth a virgin, so shall thy sons marry thee: and as the bridegroom rejoiceth over the bride, so shall thy God rejoice over thee." So they also shall be the crown of rejoicing to faithful ministers, especially such souls whose salvation they, by their faithful labors, have been the instruments of. 1 Thessalonians 2:19-

20, "For what is our hope, or joy, or crown of rejoicing? Are not even ye in the presence of our Lord Jesus Christ at his coming? For ye are our glory and joy."

NOTES

1   For an extensive treatment of Edwards's dismissal, see David D. Hall, "Editor's Introduction," in Edwards, *Ecclesiastical Writings*, ed. Hall, Vol. 12 of *Works of Jonathan Edwards* (New Haven, CT: Yale University Press, 1994), 1-90.

2   See Edwards's letter to Reverend John Erskine, July 7, 1752, in Edwards, *Letters and Personal Writings*, ed. George S. Claghorn, Vol. 16 of *Works of Jonathan Edwards* (New Haven, CT: Yale University Press, 1998), 493.

3   John Langdon Sibley, *Biographical Sketches of Graduates of Harvard University, in Cambridge, Massachusetts* (Cambridge, MA: Charles William Sever, 1873), 27.

4   For a discussion of Edwards's "cannibalization" of his sermons, see Wilson H. Kimnach, "Jonathan Edwards' Art of Prophesying," in Edwards, *Sermons and Discourses 1720-1723*, ed. Kimnach, Vol. 10 of *Works of Jonathan Edwards* (New Haven, CT: Yale University Press, 1992), 159-163.

5   In July 1756 Edwards re-preached this sermon for the ordination of Cornelius Jones in Sandisfield, Massachusetts, a community first known as Houstonic Township No. 3. In a conversation with him, Ken Minkema not only identified Cornelius Jones, but he also affirmed the likelihood of "No. 3" referring to the community of Sandisfield.

6   Conjectural rendering due to the poor state of the manuscript.

7   Edwards wrote, "of the will of God."

8   Edwards deleted with a vertical line: "If ministers imitate Christ in his labors, self-denial, and sufferings for the good of men's souls they."

SCRIPTURE INDEX

GENERAL INDEX